90-0788

WITHDRAWN

# TRADING WITH CANADA

A Twentieth Century Fund Paper

# TRADING WITH CANADA

## The Canada-U.S. Free Trade Agreement

## BY GILBERT R. WINHAM

**PP** Priority Press Publications/New York/1988

**Library of Congress Cataloging-in-Publication Data**
Winham, Gilbert R.
  Trading with Canada
  "A Twentieth century fund paper."
  Bibliography, p.
  Includes index.
  1. Tariff—Law and legislation—Canada.
2. Duty-free importation—Law and legislation—Canada.
3. Tariff—Law and legislation—United States.
4. Duty-free importation—Law and legislation—United
States. I. Title.
KF6668.C326W56   1988     343.7105'6     88-31676
ISBN 0-87078-251-7          347.10356
ISBN 0-87078-250-9 (pbk.)

# Foreword

Reports of the increasingly heated debate in Canada over the bilateral free trade agreement concluded last spring between the United States and Canada have provided many Americans with an opportunity to better understand their neighbor to the north. As the current outcry in Canada suggests, the removal of trade barriers between the two countries involves more than economic questions. With the American market accounting for some three-fourths of Canada's exports and imports, the prospect of free trade with the United States has many attractive features for Canadians. But at the same time, some believe that free trade poses a threat to Canada's economic self-sufficiency and, more importantly, its perceived independence.

Both reactions have been amply displayed in recent months. While Canadian government advocates of the bill argue that the market competition created by the agreement will be a significant spur to the Canadian economy, opposition leaders insist that removing trade barriers will only increase Canada's deep dependence on the U.S. economy. (One Canadian politican warned that the free trade agreement, if enacted, could turn Canada into America's fifty-first state within twenty-five years.) In fact, both federal opposition parties in Canada have come out against the agreement, and as of this writing, it seems likely that they will soon force an election.

The Twentieth Century Fund is not a newcomer to the area of U.S.-Canadian relations. In 1965, it supported George W. Wilson, Scott Gordon, and Stanislaw Judek's *Canada: An Appraisal of Its Needs and Resources.* But much has changed since then, and we believe that Gilbert Winham's paper is an auspicious new beginning for us in this area. A professor and former chairman of the department of political science at Dalhousie University in Canada, author of *International Trade and the Tokyo Round Negotiations,* and a member of the staff of the Macdonald Royal Commission on the Economy, Winham is well equipped to analyze both the political and economic aspects of the bilateral agreement.

After examining the history of the negotiations and analyzing the areas that were most troublesome to negotiate, Winham goes on to argue that while a rejection of the agreement would be a lost opportunity for the United States, for Canada, it would have far more serious consequences. Nevertheless, he is sensitive to the complex issues surrounding Canada's concern for its sovereignty. His paper is both useful and informative, and we at the Fund are grateful to him for it.

Marcia Bystryn, ACTING DIRECTOR
The Twentieth Century Fund
September 1988

# Table of Contents

# Acknowledgments

I began writing this short book for the Twentieth Century Fund more than a year ago. It explains how the Canada-U.S. Free Trade Agreement was negotiated, and what it will mean for the two countries. It is based on available public documents, and on confidential interviews with twenty-three Canadian officials and eleven U.S. officials who participated in negotiating the Agreement. I am grateful to these individuals for making their time available to me.

I wish to thank particularly Judith Hippler Bello of the Office of the U.S. Trade Representative and Michael Hart of the Trade Negotiations Office, Ottawa, who read and commented on an early version of the manuscript. Clearly, neither they nor their offices are responsible for the final product. Others who read and offered advice on the text include Linda Winham, Florian Bail, and Robert Finbow. I appreciate the criticism I received, and did the best I could with it.

Luke Ashworth served as research assistant for this project, Nina Winham provided editorial assistance, and Paulette Chiasson prepared successive drafts of the manuscript, often under considerable time pressure. Finally, Beverly Goldberg, assistant director of the Twentieth Century Fund, provided many helpful suggestions on style and content in the course of editing the entire manuscript. I appreciate the efforts of these individuals, and feel lucky to have worked with them.

# Preface

In a dramatic eleventh-hour agreement reached on October 3, 1987, Canada and the United States concluded a trade deal that will substantially reduce bilateral trade restrictions and increase competition in the private sector. This agreement symbolizes the changing economic relationship between these two countries, and it is designed to move that relationship from the fractious disputes of the 1970s to greater government cooperation (along with marketplace competition) in the 1980s.

In Canada, the free trade agreement (FTA) has the utmost political visibility. The Conservative government of Prime Minister Brian Mulroney took an uncharacteristic, bold initiative in foreign policy in proposing the agreement to the United States. Both Federal opposition parties have vowed to defeat the FTA in the next election, and the Liberal government in Canada's largest province, Ontario, has refused to support it. Canadian nationalists from across the political spectrum have denounced the deal as a sell-out to the Yanks. For example, National Democratic party (NDP) leader Ed Broadbent has claimed it will turn Canada into America's fifty-first state in twenty-five years. Meanwhile in the United States, the FTA is seen as an important blow by the Reagan administration against the protectionist forces that have dominated Washington trade politics during this decade. The Canada initiative is also seen as a bold first step in a new, much larger effort to open trade with all countries. As *The New York Times* editorialized: "Today Canada; tomorrow the world."

Both in how it was negotiated and in what it means, the Canada-U.S. trade deal is a political story of great interest. Even the most detached academic judgment would conclude that this negotiation has been the most important single feature of the North American relationship in re-

1

cent memory. At stake in the FTA is the trade policy regime that governs over $130 billion of two-way trade, which is the largest bilateral trade flow between members of the General Agreement on Tariffs and Trade (GATT). Also at stake may be the economic and political stability of one of the world's most durable alliances.

The FTA is obviously an important issue for Canada, as indicated by the massive coverage this issue receives in Canadian newspapers. It is also important for the United States. Canada is America's largest trading partner, and even though the economic relationship may not be as troublesome as the one with Japan, it is a critical trade link for the U.S. economy. For its part, Canada relies on the United States for about three-fourths of its international trade. The reality of the North American economic relationship is bilateral, and the efforts to negotiate a bilateral trade agreement have simply been an attempt to bring the political regime into line with economic reality.

The FTA will have an impact on the multilateral trade system, as well as U.S. and Canadian policies toward that system. The elements of the Agreement were far-reaching, and included services, investment, and energy—areas not normally part of trade negotiations. Both nations learned a great deal from negotiating these subjects, and some have claimed the results will serve as a model for the multilateral trade negotiation (Uruguay Round) now being conducted in the GATT. An examination of the FTA and the process that led to it brings a better understanding of the U.S.-Canadian economic relationship and the effect that relationship will have on the broader international economic system.

# Chapter 1
# History

$F$ree trade has a long history in U.S.-Canadian relations. The background of this issue reveals much about the economic relationship between Canada and the United States, and about the problems modern negotiators face in reaching a bilateral agreement. The earliest embodiment of free trade between Canada and the United States was the Reciprocity Treaty of 1854.[1] The 1854 treaty was pursued by Canada as a reaction to the movement by Britain toward free trade embodied in the repeal of the Corn Laws in 1846.* In response to the Canadian action, Britain withdrew imperial preferences to Canada, causing Canada to turn its attention southward to the manufacturing strength of the United States.

Thus, in the late 1840s, Canada sought negotiations for a trade treaty in the context of a world economic depression. Hard times in Canada brought talk of annexation to the United States, but this sentiment receded in favor of a search for new markets and new capital.

Negotiations for the Reciprocity Treaty took eight years, and the Canadian government found it difficult to arouse much interest in it in the United States. But Canadian persistence paid off, and a limited free trade agreement was finally concluded as part of the Elgin-Marcy Treaty of 1854.

The goods included under the Reciprocity Treaty were mainly natural products, including meat and dairy, fish, ores and minerals, forest products, and sundry agricultural goods. Manufactured products (with the exception of dyestuffs and rags) were largely excluded, due to the im-

---

* In modern times, Canada had a similar reaction when Britain decided to join the Common Market: it turned its attention to its North American economic relationship.

portance of tariffs on manufactures for government revenues. Despite being limited to natural products, the Reciprocity Treaty did place most Canada-U.S. trade on a duty free basis. Estimates suggest that about 55 percent of U.S. imports into the Province of Canada (including modern-day Ontario and Quebec) were duty free, as against 90 percent of Canadian imports into the United States.[2] The terms of the treaty were carefully drawn to benefit different sections of both countries. For example, grains, ores, and meat were of interest to the Great Lakes regions, while maritimers gained markets in fish, lumber, and coal in exchange for fishing rights for the Americans.

Trade flourished under the Reciprocity Treaty, although there were numerous complaints from both sides about violations of the accord. In 1866, the United States unilaterally abrogated the treaty, in part because of certain tariff increases on manufactured goods in Canada that were not covered by the treaty, but mostly because of ill feeling generated toward Canada during the Civil War. This action left an unfortunate legacy in Canada. Today, even at the highest levels, doubts are occasionally expressed about whether the United States could be counted on to carry through with an economic treaty with Canada. The fact that Canada is not a major factor in the U.S. economy makes it difficult to dispel these doubts completely.

The period 1854–66 coincided with an economic boom in Canada, which was probably due more to a natural upturn of the business cycle than to the effects of the Reciprocity Treaty. Nevertheless, the period was remembered warmly in Canada. With the British North America Act of 1867, the separate colonies of Canada confederated into an independent nation. Attempts were again made by the government of Canada in 1869, 1871, and 1874 to negotiate a new trade agreement. These attempts were widely supported in Canada, but there was little interest in the United States,[3] particularly in Congress, where the Canadian initiatives were perceived as being inconsistent with the protectionist principle that underlay U.S. tariff legislation.

Five years later, a new government under Sir John A. MacDonald brought in the National Policy of 1879 on an appeal to nationalism and protectionism. This policy of high tariffs was intended to promote manufacturing in Canada, and it was a conscious reaction to the U.S. rejection of efforts at free trade. Indeed, the policy was in part aimed at the United States, for MacDonald argued that it was only by restricting American trade that the United States would be induced to accept reciprocity with Canada. As MacDonald put it: "[The United States] will not have anything like reciprocity of trade with us unless we show them that it will be to their advantage. . . . It is only by closing our doors and by cutting them out of our markets, that they will open theirs to us."[4] As these events are viewed from a modern perspective, it is important to recognize that Canada—which today is a high tariff country among nations of the Organization for Economic Cooperation and Development (OECD)—arguably did not turn to protectionism by choice. Rather, it was the absence of opportunity to establish a more liberal regime with its larger neighbor that started Canada down the road to high protection.

The subsequent history of the National Policy offers a textbook case of the political effects of economic protectionism. Most of Canada's manufacturing sector grew up under this policy, and these interests came to see the trade protectionism of the National Policy as an immutable part of the economic environment. Business supported protectionism, thus politicizing the trade issue in a way that was previously unknown in Canada.[5] The national election of 1891 was fought largely on a Liberal platform calling for "unrestricted reciprocity," and MacDonald, invoking Canadian nationalism and the Empire connection, handily won the contest.

Free trade (or reciprocity, as the term has been used in Canada) re-emerged in the election of 1911. On a U.S. initiative, a reciprocity agreement had been negotiated by the Laurier government, and it became the principal issue in the subsequent election. Manufacturing and financial interests again took strong exception to this plan, becoming exceptionally active in the electoral campaign. The antireciprocity forces made blatant appeals to Canadian nationalism, and by extension, to anti-Americanism. These appeals received widespread support. Laurier lost the election to Borden of the Conservatives, and although there were other issues at stake, it was widely regarded as a defeat for reciprocity and closer relations with the United States.

The Canadian government again made efforts at the ministerial level in 1922 and 1923 to interest the United States in trade negotiations. These made little progress, as the United States was then moving in the direction of more and not less protectionism. In the 1920s and 1930s, little action was taken, except that in 1935 and 1938, Canada and the United States concluded two bilateral agreements pursuant to the Reciprocal Trade Agreements Act of 1934.[6] These agreements were limited and were not reciprocity agreements in the earlier sense; nevertheless, they constituted the first commercial agreements between the two countries since the 1854 Reciprocity Agreement. Finally, in 1947-48, on the initiative of the U.S. government, Prime Minister Mackenzie King authorized a secret negotiation of several months' duration to draw up a comprehensive free trade agreement. In the end, in part because of the uncertainties of the approval process in the United States, King formally decided not to proceed and talks were broken off. That was the last time a comprehensive trade deal was seriously considered by either country.

The only major success in the long-standing effort to negotiate bilateral trade was the Canada-U.S. Automotive Products Trade Agreement of 1965. In the late 1950s, the Canadian auto industry (a branch-plant replica of the U.S. industry) suffered a crisis of decreasing productivity and increasing product prices. The industry operated behind high tariff walls, and the difficulties were diagnosed as inadequate market size accompanied by low-volume production. In an effort to increase market size, the Canadian government initiated a duty-remission program that effectively allowed manufacturers to avoid paying duties on imported autos and parts to the extent that they increased exports to the United States. This program was argued to be an unfair subsidy by U.S. auto parts manufacturers, and it attracted a countervailing duty suit. In an effort to avoid this dispute, the two countries negotiated the auto agreement.[7]

The agreement liberalized trade by removing tariffs on all original equipment parts and vehicles, but it contained a number of investment safeguards: it required auto manufacturers to maintain investment in Canada and to ensure that vehicles assembled in Canada met specified targets for Canadian content. The auto agreement was generally regarded as successful; trade in this sector has increased by twenty-four times since 1965, and now accounts for more than one-third of all U.S.-Canadian trade.[8] As a model for future agreements, the auto agreement was attractive because of its liberalizing effect on trade, but the investment safeguards remained controversial on the American side.

Looking back, it becomes clear that, caught between the attraction of the U.S. economy on the one hand and the difficulties of establishing a viable national economy in Canada on the other hand, successive Canadian governments have returned to the idea of securing a wide-ranging reciprocity agreement with the United States. Free trade was less popular with the business community and the public once the protectionism of the National Policy had worked its full effects; nevertheless, the idea remained attractive. One of the important facts about the current situation is that the Canadian business community, for its own economic reasons, has became far more supportive of freer trade than it was even a decade ago. The FTA has indeed raised nationalist opposition in Canada, but the automatic link between business interests and nationalism seems to have been broken.

A second conclusion is that, with few exceptions, Canadians have found it difficult to attract enthusiasm in the United States for the idea of reciprocal free trade. This failure may have been due to the inherent difficulties of a small state proposing initiatives to a larger partner, or it may have been a matter of inappropriate timing. Given that the United States has a much larger home market and a much smaller dependence on foreign trade, an agreement with Canada never seemed to have enough economic value to be worth the administrative and political costs incurred in its negotiation. Today, U.S. indifference toward Canada has lessened; nevertheless, one of the central dramas of the free trade negotiation was the inherent tension between a larger, more distracted party and a smaller, highly interested, and inherently conflicted party. As seen from the Canadian side, the danger was that Canada appeared to have to go a considerable distance in the negotiation to attract interest on the U.S. side, but this strategy, if carried too far, risked being counterproductive at home.

A third conclusion from the history of reciprocity talks is that in economic terms, and even politically, Canadians tend to define themselves in relation to the United States. The U.S. economy is seen as attractive as well as threatening to Canada, and the same could probably be said for American society in general. This view creates conflict in Canada, which is made worse by the fact that free trade has always brought out Canadian nationalism. As a result, public debate in Canada often attributes cataclysmic results to trade agreements—results wholly unrelated to the technical issues covered in those agreements. Such overstatement is unavoidable because, for better or worse, any major agreement with the United States touches on how Canadians think about themselves. By negotiating a bilateral trade agreement with the United States, the Canadian government—in the eyes of the Opposition—has weakened Canadian identity and has reduced Canada's stature from an international actor to a regional actor. The politics of this symbolic issue are bound to be sharp and distracting.

# Chapter 2
# The Road to Negotiation

**Economic Structure**

The United States and Canada share many characteristics. Both countries were settled from abroad, and in the words of American political philosopher Louis Hartz, both were "born free." Both countries absorbed immigrants from many different countries; in Canada, the result is a nation with two founding races and two official languages, a nation with a regional diversity reflective in large part of the settlement patterns of Canada's immigrants. Both the Canadian and American peoples pushed their domain from the Atlantic to the Pacific, and created an integrated economy and polity from coast to coast. In Canada, this process was much more difficult, for against the efforts to integrate the country from East to West there was always the strong pull southward of the large and vital American workplace. Finally, both countries faced and solved problems of democratic government, and evolved similar federal structures coupled with representative governments at the national and regional levels.

The two countries differ in that the United States quickly developed a strong, self-sufficient economy, while Canada's domestic economy has always been defined largely by its relationship to the international economy. The difference was a result of Canada's smaller population, which was never a sufficient internal market for the development of efficient manufacturing. Instead, trade with the "mother countries" of Canada's immigrants and with the industrial centers in Europe and the United States sustained economic activity in Canada, and in turn shaped the demographic patterns and institutions of the country.[1]

In economic terms, Canada is the most trade-dependent of the major OECD nations, as reflected in the fact that today foreign exports account for over 30 percent of Canada's gross national product. (Figure 1 compares Canada's export/GNP ratio for all goods and services with selected OECD countries; Table 1 provides data for a similar comparison for merchandise exports.) By contrast, the United States is the least trade-dependent of this group. The consequences of these differences have been seen historically in the response of these two countries to hard times. In periods of economic distress, Canadians have tended to look outward to deal with internal problems, and to seek their salvation in international trading relations. On the other hand, the United States could not expect to make major repairs in its economy by external measures. In hard times, Americans have been more likely to look inward, seeking their salvation in the revitalization of the domestic economy. Admittedly, the position of the United States in economic policy is less independent than it once was, but nevertheless the North American partners remain substantially different on this dimension. One result of these differences is that it has been hard to find the right mix of economic conditions that would lead both countries to conclude a bilateral trade agreement.[2]

### Table 1
### Ratio of Merchandise Exports to Gross Domestic Product
### (percent)

|  | 1965 | 1970 | 1973 | 1974 | 1975 | 1979 | 1980 |
|---|---|---|---|---|---|---|---|
| United States | 3.9 | 4.4 | 5.5 | 7.0 | 6.9 | 7.5 | 8.4 |
| Japan | 9.5 | 9.8 | 9.0 | 12.2 | 11.2 | 10.3 | 12.4 |
| West Germany | 15.6 | 18.4 | 19.6 | 23.4 | 21.4 | 22.6 | 23.6 |
| France | 10.2 | 12.5 | 14.3 | 17.1 | 15.4 | 17.1 | 17.1 |
| United Kingdom | 13.3 | 15.9 | 17.3 | 20.2 | 19.1 | 22.4 | 22.0 |
| Canada | 15.6 | 19.5 | 20.2 | 21.6 | 19.6 | 24.2 | 25.6 |
| Italy | 12.3 | 14.3 | 15.7 | 19.5 | 18.1 | 22.3 | 19.7 |
| EEC[a] (including intra-community trade) | 15.2 | 18.1 | 20.0 | 23.8 | 21.3 | 23.4 | 23.6 |
| EEC[a] (excluding intra-community trade) | 8.2 | 9.0 | 9.5 | 11.7 | 10.8 | 10.9 | 11.1 |
| OECD | 9.0 | 10.6 | 12.4 | 14.9 | 14.2 | 15.4 | 16.5 |

a. Adjusted to include all the present members of the European Community.
*Source: A Review of Canadian Trade Policy* (Ottawa: Department of External Affairs, 1983), p. 20.

**Figure 1**
**Exports of Goods and Services by Country**
**(as percentage of gross national product) 1960 and 1980**

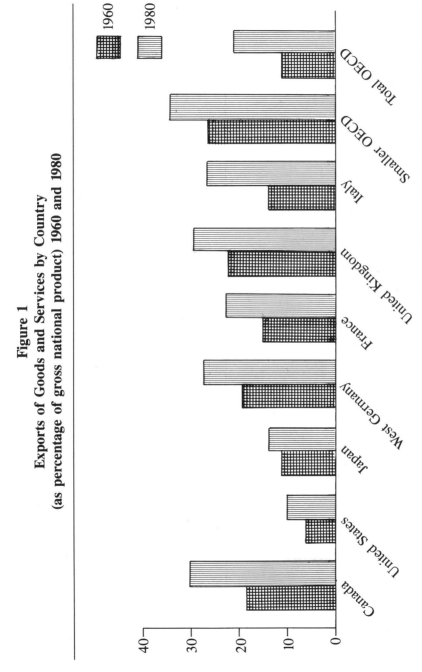

*Source: Report of the Royal Commission on the Economic Union and Development Prospects for Canada, Volume 1, 1985, p. 235.*

In the colonial period, Canada was situated on the margin of European civilization, and its economic relations with the center were driven by its exports of staples: fish, fur, and, later, timber and wheat. As the nation grew and technology changed, Canada's minerals and ores were developed for export to more highly industrialized nations. Today, Canada is a fully industrialized nation producing a wide range of manufactured goods, but it continues to have a resource-based economy and its comparative advantage lies in semimanufactured goods fabricated from natural resources (see Table 2).

Canada has an international economic profile that is analogous to some resource-exporting developing countries. Furthermore, it has suffered from some of the same problems of the developing countries, such as a high proportion of foreign investment and ownership in the total economy, and uncertainties in the foreign demand for resource-based products. In these matters, Canada's history differs from that of its larger neighbor, for the manufacturing strength of the United States has made it a more resilient actor in the world economy. In the 1980s, the demand for Canada's resource-based exports has been depressed, putting even more pressure on Canada to increase the competitiveness of its manufacturing sector and to extend the processing of resource-based products beyond the primary and semimanufactured stages.

Canada and the United States also have a different history regarding the role of the state in the economy. In Canada, governments, both federal and provincial, are important players in the economy, and this fact is reflected in levels of government support (see Table 3). Data on government support are controversial, for there are no commonly accepted definitions or measurements for government subsidies. Nevertheless, published data tend to show that the level of Canadian subsidies is consistent with other OECD countries, but different from the United States, where subsidy levels are lower. Other data suggest that the difference between Canada and the United States has been growing in recent years.[3]

The role of government in the economy is a historical fact in Canada. Because Canada traditionally exported raw materials, the Canadian government became closely involved in economic activity through providing transportation, finance, and other support services. It spent heavily on railroads and canals, and provided grants and subsidies to support other infrastructural development. Government involvement in the economy began in earliest colonial times with the trade in fur and fish, and the pattern reinforced itself with each new staple commodity Canadians produced. In the United States, in contrast, the economy, driven

**Table 2**
**Canada's Domestic Merchandise Exports**
**Percentage Distribution by Major Commodity Group**[a]

|  | Food, Feed, Beverages, and Tobacco[b] | Inedible Crude Materials | Inedible Fabricated Materials | Finished Manufactured Goods | |
|---|---|---|---|---|---|
|  |  |  |  | Automotive | Total |
| 1960 | 18.8 | 21.2 | 51.9 | 7.8 | 1.3 |
| 1961 | 22.0 | 20.8 | 48.3 | 8.8 | 0.8 |
| 1962 | 20.1 | 22.0 | 47.1 | 10.6 | 0.9 |
| 1963 | 21.5 | 21.0 | 45.7 | 11.5 | 1.3 |
| 1964 | 2.7 | 20.0 | 43.3 | 13.7 | 2.2 |
| 1965 | 20.0 | 20.7 | 43.7 | 15.3 | 4.2 |
| 1966 | 19.5 | 19.3 | 39.8 | 21.0 | 9.9 |
| 1967 | 14.8 | 19.0 | 38.0 | 28.0 | 15.6 |
| 1968 | 12.1 | 18.5 | 36.4 | 32.7 | 20.6 |
| 1969 | 10.1 | 17.1 | 35.7 | 36.8 | 24.3 |
| 1970 | 11.4 | 18.8 | 35.8 | 33.8 | 21.3 |
| 1971 | 2.1 | 18.8 | 33.3 | 35.6 | 24.0 |
| 1972 | 12.0 | 18.1 | 33.4 | 36.3 | 24.0 |
| 1973 | 12.7 | 20.2 | 33.1 | 33.8 | 21.8 |
| 1974 | 12.2 | 24.6 | 33.8 | 29.2 | 18.0 |
| 1975 | 12.7 | 24.5 | 30.4 | 32.2 | 19.8 |
| 1976 | 11.4 | 22.0 | 32.5 | 33.8 | 21.8 |
| 1977 | 10.5 | 20.3 | 34.2 | 34.9 | 23.9 |
| 1978 | 10.1 | 16.9 | 36.7 | 36.1 | 24.0 |
| 1979 | 9.8 | 19.5 | 37.9 | 32.5 | 18.5 |
| 1980 | 11.1 | 19.8 | 39.4 | 29.4 | 14.7 |
| 1981 | 11.6 | 18.7 | 37.6 | 31.2 | 16.1 |

a. Shares will not sum to 100 percent because of the omission of special transactions which accounted for 0.2 to 0.4 percent of the total over the whole period.
b. Including live animals.
N.B.: The weakness of Canada's exports of finished manufactured goods, other than automotive products which go almost exclusively to the United States, is clearly evident.
*Source: A Review of Canadian Trade Policy* (Ottawa: Department of External Affairs, 1983), p. 26.

by a large domestic market, developed far more independently of the influence of government. Furthermore, American political values came to accept a strict separation between business and government that has no real counterpart in Canadian values. It is often said that Americans trust the market and fear government and that Canadians trust government and fear the market: while this is an overstatment, it does summarize the different historical experience and outlook of the two peoples.

Canada has experimented with an industrial policy since the colonial period. Governments have pursued policies to promote the growth of manufacturing, so that Canadians could avoid the condition, as it was popularly expressed, of being "hewers of wood and drawers of water." These policies bore some similarities to those currently being pursued by governments in the developing countries in South America and elsewhere. In Canada, the cornerstone of these efforts was the National Policy of 1879. This policy instituted a protective tariff for Canadian manufacturing, which had the added effect of inducing American manufacturers to locate plant and investments in Canada. That this effect was intended was made clear by the Canadian minister of finance in 1904, speaking in defense of Canada's tariff levels:

### Table 3
### Government Current Operating Subsidies
### and Aid to Private Capital Formation in Six Major AICs
### 1976 and 1979 (percentage of GNP)

|  | 1976 | | | 1979 | | |
|---|---|---|---|---|---|---|
|  | Current Account[a] | Capital Formation[b] | Total | Current Account | Capital Formation | Total |
| United States | 0.3 | 0.1 | 0.4 | 0.4 | 0.2 | 0.6 |
| Canada | 1.7 | 0.9 | 2.6 | 1.7 | 0.5 | 2.2 |
| Japan | 1.3 | 0.1 | 1.4 | 1.3 | 0.2 | 1.5 |
| France | 2.1 | 0.6 | 2.7 | 2.0 | 0.4 | 2.4 |
| West Germany | 1.5 | 0.3 | 1.8 | 1.8 | 0.3 | 2.1 |
| United Kingdom | 2.8 | 0.9 | 3.7 | 2.3 | 0.6 | 2.9 |

a. Payments reported on national accounts, including direct payments to private sector companies and operating losses of public corporations.
b. Includes direct grants and credits.
*Source:* Peter Morici, *The Global Competitive Struggle: Challenges to the United States and Canada* (Toronto and Washington: Canadian-American Committee, 1984), p. 26; reprinted by permission.

I think, Sir, as to whether or not it is adequate protection we have some evidence of a gratifying character that the tariff, without being excessive, is high enough to bring some American industries across the line and a tariff which is able to bring these industries into Canada looks very much like a tariff which affords adequate protection.[4]

The protection established by the National Policy remained essentially unchanged until the negotiation of the FTA. Canada used tariffs

### Table 4
### Tariffs by Industrial Sector, Post-Tokyo Round
### (percentage)

|  | Canada | United States |
|---|---|---|
| Textiles | 16.9 | 7.2 |
| Clothing | 23.7 | 18.4 |
| Leather products | 4.0 | 2.5 |
| Footwear | 21.5 | 9.0 |
| Wood products | 2.5 | 0.2 |
| Furniture and fixtures | 14.3 | 4.6 |
| Paper products | 6.6 | 0.0 |
| Printing and publishing | 1.1 | 0.3 |
| Chemicals | 7.9 | 0.6 |
| Petroleum products | 0.4 | 0.0 |
| Rubber products | 7.3 | 3.2 |
| Nonmetal mineral products | 4.4 | 0.3 |
| Glass products | 6.9 | 5.7 |
| Iron and steel | 5.1 | 2.7 |
| Nonferrous metals | 3.3 | 0.5 |
| Metal products | 8.6 | 4.0 |
| Nonelectrical machinery | 4.6 | 2.2 |
| Electrical machinery | 7.5 | 4.5 |
| Transportation equipment | 0.0 | 0.0 |
| Miscellaneous manufactures | 5.0 | 0.9 |

Note: Canadian tariff averages are weighted by imports from the United States, and vice versa.
*Source:* Paul Wonnacott, *The United States and Canada: The Quest for Free Trade* (Washington, D.C.: Institute for International Economics, 1987), p. 4.

as a means of promoting industrial development, and generally maintained higher levels than the United States through a series of postwar tariff-cutting negotiations under the GATT. Even after the tariff cuts mandated by the Tokyo Round, tariff levels in all sectors remained higher than those of the United States (see Table 4).

In terms of overall tariff levels, U.S. average tariffs on dutiable imports after 1987 were approximately 4 to 5 percent, although on imports from Canada the average was much lower—about 1 percent—because of tariff-free trade under the automotive agreement and the high level of duty-free resource imports. By comparison, Canadian average tariffs on dutiable imports after 1987 averaged about 9 to 10 percent.[5] To put these figures in perspective, however, it must be recalled that after 1987 about 80 percent of Canadian exports entered the United States duty free, while the comparable figure for U.S. exports into Canada was about 65 percent. What these figures mean for Canada is that about two-thirds of imports from the United States entered duty free, while the remaining one-third carried duties averaging about 9 percent.

## Incentives to Negotiate

Since World War II, both the United States and Canada have pursued what is essentially a multilateral trade policy within the GATT. This policy was a result of an enormous initiative on the part of the United States, which, as the leading Western economic power, was largely responsible for the creation of the liberal GATT regime. As a trade-dependent middle power, Canada also supported multilateral trade liberalization under the GATT, but it had always managed to pursue multilateralism without losing the margin of protection inherent in the National Policy of 1879. Canada's postwar trade policy served it well, and the country participated fully in the long period of international economic growth that stretched from the late 1940s to the oil shocks of the early 1970s.

The 1970s were turbulent economic times for Canada, as well as other nations; this period was followed by the recession of 1981-82, by far the most severe postwar recession for Canada. The recession shook the then-Liberal government of Pierre Trudeau, which responded by creating a national Royal Commission to inquire into the sources of Canada's difficulties and make recommendations for future economic policy. Under the Honorable Donald Macdonald, the work of the commission—a major reevaluation—was the largest effort of its kind in Canadian history.

The commission presented its findings in September 1985 in a massive three-volume report. One of its main—and certainly most politically visible—recommendations was for Canada to negotiate bilateral free trade with the United States. In retrospect, it seems unusual that a national commission charged with such broad responsibilities would make its most significant recommendation in the foreign policy area; certainly an equivalent commission in the United States would be unlikely to reach a similar conclusion. The reasoning of the Macdonald Commission is important to an understanding of Canada's initiative for a free trade negotiation.

The commission noted that in certain respects the Canadian economy had reached a turning point. First, Canada traditionally had a resource-based economy, and trade in resource products (or "rocks and logs") had been the backbone of Canada's export position. However, international markets for these products were depressed, and the prospects for future growth were limited. The commission stated: ". . .it is likely that the resource sector as a whole will continue to decline . . . [and] output is unlikely to grow as quickly as that for manufactured goods and services so that the share of GNP attributed to these activities will fall further."[6] Regarding international trade, the commission concluded: ". . . this [resource] trade orientation will increasingly need to be supplemented by more highly processed products in order to maintain our access to the goods and services of other nations."[7]

Turning to an analysis of manufacturing performance, the commission noted disquieting signs that Canada's performance had fallen behind most OECD countries in the previous decade. Most worrisome was Canada's poor performance relative to the United States, which had been painfully revealed during the 1981-82 recession. In the United States, real gross national expenditure (GNE) fell by about 2 percent between 1981 and 1982, and the unemployment rate rose by 2 percent. In Canada, the fall of GNE was 4.2 percent, and the increase in unemployment 4.4 percent. The commission noted that many Canadians feared that unemployment levels would never return to the pre-1981-82 levels in affected industries, and it emphasized the importance of improving productivity throughout the economy, and especially in the manufacturing sector. The commission concluded: "If productivity growth were to stay at the low level of the past decade, Canadians could not look forward to any appreciable further gains in their standard of living."[8]

Finally, turning to international trade, the commission noted the growing importance of the United States for Canadian trade. Canada had long been dependent on imports of goods from the United States, but an important change had occurred in Canada's export dependency over the past thirty years. Despite the efforts of the Canadian government in the

1970s to diversify trade (known as the "Third Option" policy), Canadian trade had become through natural forces more oriented to the U.S. market. Moreover, exports to the United States also included products with the highest manufactured content—such as automobiles and machinery—in Canada's total exports, and therefore the United States represented a market that Canada hoped to expand in the future. In its analyses of Canada's policy alternatives, the commission emphasized the goal of increased productivity, which was to be achieved through greater economic competition and a reliance on market forces. It stated: "The stimulation of competition is the key to economic growth and productivity improvement"; and ". . . we Canadians must significantly increase our reliance on market forces."[9] This goal was to be accomplished through an industrial policy that would provide a rationale for government action and would also replace the inappropriate National Policy of 1879. In its discussion of industrial policy, the commission focused on international trade, and again it revealed the importance of the international economy to Canada's domestic economic policy. The commission stated: "The question of whether to opt for free trade or for protectionism is undoubtedly the key issue to be resolved in forming an industrial policy."[10] Free trade had the potential, in the commission's opinion, to create ". . . a fundamental change in the relationship of the state to the market";[11] and in the following statement, the commission left no doubt in which direction it believed that change should occur:

> We are saying, in short, that a key component of Canada's industrial policy should be a commitment to freer trade, which should be matched by a freer flow of capital investment than there has been over the past decade or so.[12]

The commissioners ideally viewed free trade as a multilateral concept, but they quickly bowed to practicality by calling initially for a bilateral agreement with the United States. The commission argued that an FTA with the United States would increase the security of access to U.S. markets by making Canadian exports less susceptible to U.S. nontariff measures (NTMs). The NTMs in question were U.S. countervailing, antidumping, and safeguarding actions that had since 1980 been applied to Canadian exports ranging from lumber to fish to speciality steel and hogs. The actions created trade and hence investment uncertainties on the Canadian side, and were seen as especially threatening given Canada's high dependence on U.S. trade and the likelihood that this dependence might even increase in future years.

In addition, the commission held that free trade would improve the access to the U.S. market. While this market was already substantially tariff free, there were important areas such as petroleum or quality apparel where U.S. duties restricted access of Canadian exporters. Canada was viewed by the commission as the only major industrial nation without free access to a market of over 100 million persons, and a bilateral agreement with the United States was seen as the most expedient way to gain such access.

Finally, the commission claimed that the most important reason for free trade was that it would improve productivity and competitiveness in Canada's manufacturing sector, which was too small to be competitive by international standards. Free trade would increase the specialization and rationalization of the Canadian economy, and thereby increase the ability of Canada's exporters to sell to Americans and to the outside world. This argument firmly linked free trade with the commission's central concern for increasing Canada's competitiveness, and it overturned entirely the legacy of the National Policy of 1879. As the commission summarized: "In our view, a commitment to freer trade—on a multilateral basis if possible, but at least with the United States—would provide the single most important incentive for private enterprise in Canada to become more efficient, more innovative and, hence, more competitive."[13]

The report of the Macdonald Commission was embraced by the Conservative government of Brian Mulroney because it reflected the philosophy and broader concerns of that government. That philosophy placed an emphasis on increased reliance on market forces in the economy, which was not unlike the philosophy held by the Reagan administration. The document *Competitiveness and Security: Directions for Canada's International Relations,* published in the early years of the Mulroney government, made clear in no uncertain terms the importance that the government attached to economic productivity and competitiveness.[14] Moreover, just as the Macdonald Commission had done, the document linked Canada's competitiveness to international trade, which perhaps explains why an ostensibly domestic concept like economic productivity became the central focus in a government paper on foreign policy. The document stated: "Our dependence on trade means that we are economically secure only if we are internationally competitive." It concluded: "The messages are clear. Our economic interests require us to be competitive; we must trade if we are to prosper."[15]

The Macdonald Commission's recommendation for Canada-U.S. free trade was acted on by the Mulroney government, which saw it as a means to revitalize the private sector in Canada and as a method to reduce government intervention in the economy. The government also acted because of pressure from the Canadian business community to insulate Canadian exporters from unfair U.S. trade remedy actions, such as countervailing duties. Assuming that governments do not change historical policies for reasons other than profound philosophical convictions, it seems probable that the main incentive of the Mulroney government to negotiate the FTA was the opportunity to turn around the direction of Canadian economic policy. The Canadian government used the negotiation with the United States as a means to accomplish domestic reforms that might not have been possible through other means. The use of international negotiation to bring about domestic change is not uncommon; for example, the United States recently reformed its federal liquor tax policies in connection with the concessions exchanged during the Tokyo Round trade negotiation.[16]

On the U.S. side, there was no equivalent grand design for the FTA, and the incentives to negotiate were less clear. Although Canada is the largest trading partner of the United States, it accounted for less than 20 percent of total U.S. trade. Heading the list of U.S. concerns were Canadian duties, which at an average of about 9 percent were high enough to create serious impediments to U.S. exports. A second concern was a series of trade and investment "irritants" that had troubled U.S.-Canadian economic relations over the past decade, including Canadian policies on, for example, the screening and regulation of foreign investment and the treatment of foreign-owned firms under the national energy policy.[17]

Another concern was the opportunity to introduce new issues such as services and investment into international trade negotiations. Over considerable opposition from the developing countries, the United States had proposed both issues for the current multilateral GATT round, and a negotiation with Canada presented an opportunity to explore these areas with another industrialized trading partner. Finally, the Canadian negotiation was politically appealing to the Reagan administration. On the domestic front, the administration faced a Congress determined to enact protectionist trade legislation, and it saw in the negotiation with Canada an opportunity to maintain momentum for trade liberalization. Similarly, on the international front, the bilateral negotiation presented an opportunity to carry through a policy the administration had previously enunciated, namely, that in the face of foot dragging and obstructionism in multilateral trade forums, the United States was prepared to negotiate trade liberalization with any country or group of countries that wished to do so.

One issue that was vigorously debated in Canada but that also applied to the United States is why the two nations chose to negotiate bilaterally instead of multilaterally, which is the more normal procedure. For Canada, a bilateral negotiation represented a substantial departure from the multilateral character of Canada's postwar foreign policy, and it carried the risk that third parties might perceive Canada as having reduced its political independence by virtue of establishing closer economic relations with the United States. For the United States, a bilateral negotiation appeared to contradict the GATT principles of non-discrimination and universality that it had often invoked against the expansion of the preferential trading arrangements of the European Community. In both the United States and Canada, the FTA was criticized as being an unwelcome initiative in a multilateral trading system.

The move toward a bilateral negotiation on the Canadian side was motivated largely by economic realism. Proponents of the bilateral initiative emphasized that Canada's trade was substantially regional and not international and that, if trade was to be liberalized at all, it would have to be done mainly through Canada's principal trading partner. Multilateral negotiations were painfully slow because of the multiplicity of interests. Even worse, they tend to be better arenas for trade liberalization among large countries than among middle or smaller powers because trade and, especially, tariff agreements are usually exchanged between the principal suppliers of products, and there are not many goods (especially industrial products) on which middle or smaller countries will be the principal supplier. It was this situation that had bedeviled Canada's efforts to achieve reductions in U.S. petroleum tariffs during the Tokyo Round.

In the end, the Canadian government chose the bilateral route because, given Canada's trade structure and the inherent difficulty of the multilateral process, it was the only practical way to achieve a liberalization of trade. The United States, for its own reasons, made the same decision. The Reagan administration recognized that, despite its liberal rhetoric on trade, a bilateral agreement with Canada would probably represent the only trade agreement it could achieve.

To sum up, the negotiation for a U.S.-Canada FTA was a Canadian initiative and represented a fundamental change of Canadian economic policy, both domestic and toward the United States. For the United States, the issue was much less important. The U.S. government was in the position of responding to another nation's proposal for a trade negotiation, and it responded, as nations often do, by calculating costs against benefits. The United States was not motivated to see the negotiation in terms of grand strategy or of fundamental change; at most, it was an opportunity to test Canadian sincerity and perhaps to put the president's liberal rhetoric into policy. Thus, between the United States and Canada, there was an imbalance in the negotiation at its more profound levels that made the endeavor all the more difficult.

# Chapter 3
# The Negotiation Process

**Preparation for Negotiation**

The move toward free trade between the United States and Canada has an impressive intellectual history. It is an idea often explored, but never quite grasped. In the mid-1980s, the concept of free trade suddenly met with both receptive governments and a supportive business climate in the United States and Canada. But that was not enough; negotiations were needed to translate the idea into practical policy.

In any negotiation, the most important issue is whether an agreement is reached, and what effect that agreement will have on the behavior of the parties. How the agreement was reached is also important because it is often an indication of how relations between the parties will be conducted in the future. Looking back, it is clear that the free trade negotiation took on a life of its own and brought into sharp focus certain underlying problems in the economic relations of the two countries.

The negotiation started with a proposal from the Canadian government. As with most government initiatives, the Canadian decision was not sudden. Debate began in Canadian government circles after 1980 about the whole direction of Canadian trade policy, and the growing trade with the United States meant that trade with the United States figured prominently in the debate. In August 1983, the Liberal government released two documents that cautiously explored the process of negotiating freer trade with the United States within defined sectors.[1] The sector approach, as it became known, was discussed throughout the winter of 1983-84, but discarded the following summer. The approach suffered from an insurmountable limitation, namely, that each side proposed sectors where it had export interests and resisted including its weaker sectors in the negotiation. The sector initiative made clear the interests of both sides in negotiating trade, but it also demonstrated that a broader effort was necessary if any agreement were to be reached.[2]

In September 1984, Canada held a national election, which the Conservatives under Brian Mulroney won in a landslide. The Conservative government, finding the trade initiatives of the previous government to its liking, presented its own proposals, which included a comprehensive trade agreement with the United States.[3] Momentum then gathered for a negotiation with the United States.

A meeting between President Reagan and Prime Minister Mulroney (known as the "Shamrock Summit") held in March 1985 resulted in the signing of a Declaration on Trade in Goods and Services. The declaration committed both countries to improve trade relations. Further meetings of officials over the summer confirmed the feasibility of a comprehensive negotiation, and the report of the Macdonald Commission in early September provided the impetus for the government to act. Finally, on September 26, 1985, Prime Minister Mulroney announced in the House of Commons that the Canadian government would pursue a new trade agreement with the United States.

President Reagan quickly accepted the Canadian initiative, and the matter was turned over to Congress. The current framework within which the administration negotiates and Congress approves trade agreements was established by the Trade Act of 1974. Congress has the constitutional power to regulate trade, but given the fact that much trade policy is derived from negotiations with foreign countries, it is impractical to expect the administration to negotiate an international agreement and then have Congress effectively rewrite that agreement in the legislative process. To get around this problem, the trade act established a "fast-track" procedure that required the administration to consult closely with Congress during negotiation of an agreement, in return for which Congress was obliged to approve or disapprove the agreement promptly, and without making amendments. Although fast track deviates from normal legislative procedures in Congress and has been controversial, it was the basis for U.S. implementation of Tokyo Round agreements in 1979.[4]

Fast-track procedures oblige the president to notify the Senate Finance Committee and the House Ways and Means Committee of his intent to negotiate with a foreign country. The committees then have ninety legislative days (about five months) to register disapproval; if no action is taken, the negotiation can proceed. However, without warning the Senate Finance Committee scheduled a hearing on April 11, 1986, on the president's request, amid speculation that it was ready to vote down the proposal.

The Finance Committee's action precipitated ten days of crisis diplomacy within Washington, and between Ottawa and Washington as well. At the outset, it was clear that those opposed to granting authority to negotiate with Canada were in the majority. It was only through personal lobbying by the president that the situation was turned around, and on April 23, the committee voted 10-10 on a resolution to deny authority, which meant the negotiation went forward by the narrowest of margins given the rules of procedure.

The postmortems on Congress's actions revealed that the administration's request presented an opportunity to register senatorial unhappiness with the entire drift of the administration's trade policy, and particularly its alleged inattentiveness to the political problems created by the U.S. trade deficit.[5] Against this broader problem, the Canadian negotiation was seen as expendible. In addition, there was some anger directed at Canada over increased lumber exports, which were causing depressed conditions in various locations in western and southern States. Moreover, a number of senators were simply unenthusiastic about the fast-track procedure itself, and felt that any agreements negotiated by the administration should be implemented by the normal congressional legislation.

This experience could be seen as both encouraging and discouraging. On the one hand, those supporting the negotiation were relieved that Canada had not been the principal target of the Finance Committee's action. On the other hand, it was obvious that the Canadian negotiation was not a high priority with either Congress or the administration. Most distressing was the fact that the U.S. government appeared to be in disarray over trade policy, which raised doubts about its ability to focus on and close a deal with its northern neighbor.

Important preparatory steps were taken in both countries while the fast-track authority was before Congress. In Canada, where provinces are more powerful than U.S. states, a formal federal-provincial machinery was established that included regular briefings and working sessions at both official and ministerial levels.[6] Negotiating teams were also established on both sides. The prime minister appointed Simon Reisman, a retired senior official from the Department of Finance, as chief negotiator. He quickly assembled a large ad hoc organization known as the trade negotiations office (TNO), which reported directly to the cabinet. In the United States, Peter Murphy, former U.S. textile negotiator and then U.S. ambassador to the GATT, was appointed chief negotiator. For much of the negotiation, Murphy had full-time access to only one other officer—William Merkin of the U.S. Trade Representative's (USTR) Office; they had to rely on specialized help drawn from different departments of the U.S. government to cover the various areas of the negotiation.

The main difference between the Canadian and American approaches is that TNO could draw directly on vastly greater analytical resources than could the U.S. negotiating team. Furthermore, Reisman was given the political authority to cut through the normal bureaucratic resistance to new proposals, while Murphy was more dependent on the agencies from which he drew professional help. These bureaucratic differences reflected the differences in priority that Canada and the United States attached to the bilateral negotiation.

### Negotiating Stages

The first meeting between Murphy and Reisman was held on May 21-22, 1986.[7] The timetable dictated by the fast-track procedures required the president to notify Congress by October 3, 1987, of his intention to enter a trade agreement with Canada, which would allow three months for drafting relevant legislation. This would give Congress the remainder of the legislative term to act. The timetable was realistic, since the U.S. election of 1988 forced a political deadline on the talks. There were only about sixteen months in which to complete the essential elements of an agreement.

The negotiation broke down into four stages (see Table 5). The *first stage* consisted of a series of exploratory meetings during which various issues were placed on the table and work groups were formed. Initially, Canada took the position that all traditional trade issues should be on the table, including tariffs and nontariff barriers (NTBs), government procurement, and technical barriers to trade. The Canadians sought especially to negotiate an exception to U.S. unfair trade remedy laws, which had led to the application of countervailing and antidumping duties against various Canadian exports. The issues pursued by the Americans were tariffs and NTBs (particularly government subsidies), and also some of the newer trade issues such as services and intellectual property. On the sensitive matter of trade remedy law, President Reagan promised that U.S. producers would continue to have the full protection of GATT-sanctioned U.S. trade remedies. The president thereby closed the door to any blanket exceptions specific to Canada.

The first stage revealed differences in the two parties' approaches to the negotiation. Canada based its approach on the principle of "national treatment," which would have meant that Canadian goods would receive the same treatment in the United States as goods produced there, and vice versa.[8] This approach would have swept away tariffs and most other restrictions on trade, such as quotas and protectionist government procurement policies. A national treatment approach would also cut deeply into trade law. Take, for example, dumping. Dumping means selling a product abroad below its value on the domestic market. If dumping causes injury to domestic firms in a foreign country, antidumping duties can be assessed against the dumped goods by the government of the importing country. Dumping, however, has no meaning within national economies. The national treatment approach of the Canadians would have involved dropping antidumping procedures entirely between Canada and the United States. Both countries would then have been obliged to rely on existing domestic measures such as competition and antitrust policies to ensure that trade was conducted fairly across the border.

The U.S. government had no equivalent grand plan for the negotiation. It viewed the deal more as an addition to the GATT than as a new economic constitution between the two North American partners. The

## Table 5
### U.S.-Canada Free Trade Negotiations
### Negotiating Stages

| Stage | Duration | Activity |
|---|---|---|
| First | May 21, 1986 – September 28, 1986 | Preliminary meetings (5); working groups formed. |
| Second | November 12, 1986 – September 23, 1987 | Negotiation sessions (17); Canada terminates negotiation. |
| Third | September 28, 1987 – October 3, 1987 | Meetings of ministers and advisers; ad referendum agreement concluded. |
| Fourth | October 5, 1987 – December 11, 1987 | Legal drafting of final agreement; some further negotiation. |

United States did favor a large deal, particularly on tariffs, since only a large deal would conform to GATT Article XXIV, which required the parties to eliminate duties and restrictions on substantially all trade between them. The U.S. approach, however, was not based on a positive notion like national treatment. It had the rather more modest aim of getting the Canadian government to change a number of trade-related practices that had led to friction between the two countries. This approach was known as an "irritants approach," and it was a concern to Canadian negotiators and American observers as well. For example, a Canadian journalist commented on the views of Washington trade lawyer Shirley Coffield as follows:

> Yet Coffield is concerned the Administration is approaching the negotiating table in an adversarial way, mainly anxious to horse-trade a long list of Canadian trade practices that irritate Congress rather than search for innovative ways to jointly manage a huge and complex relationship.[9]

By the end of the first phase, most major issues had been looked at, and groups were formed to carry out the technical and analytical work needed to support the negotiation. Much of the work was a matter of determining constituents' positions on the various issues. For example, a preparatory meeting of representatives from industries that had complained about Canadian practices regarding copyright protection (namely, pharmaceutical and software industries) revealed that these groups were unenthusiastic about being included in a freer trade agreement with Canada. They felt they could get a better deal by negotiating directly with the Canadian government. Similarly, on government procurement, the early working group meetings received indications that the General Service Administration was opposed to a deal with Canada. Since the U.S. procurement market is ten times Canada's, U.S. negotiators argued that a deal in this area would not produce equivalent concessions.[10] This resistance was never overcome, contributing to the poor results in this area.

The negotiation was enormously complicated when on May 22, 1986, President Reagan applied an "escape clause" tariff of 35 percent for five years against Canadian cedar exports (especially, shakes and shingles). This action was taken pursuant to Article XIX of the GATT, which allows an importing country to reimpose tariffs if sharply increased imports cause serious injury to the domestic industry. In the shakes and shingles case, imports from Canada had increased their share of the U.S.

market from 40 percent in 1978 to 73 percent in 1986, while employment levels in the United States dropped from 4,531 to 2,146.[11] The U.S. administration felt obliged to help the beleaguered lumber industry, but its action infuriated Ottawa, which retaliated by raising Canadian tariffs on selected U.S. exports.

The incident provided fresh evidence of Canada's lack of secure access to the U.S. market. Some Canadian business leaders reacted by increasing the pressure on Ottawa to negotiate a dispute settlement mechanism that would prevent the unilateral application of U.S. trade remedy laws in the future.[12] Far from abating however, the difficulties created by U.S. trade remedy laws were exacerbated when U.S. lumber producers applied for countervailing duties against Canadian softwood lumber imports. The U.S. industry had lost a similar case in 1983, but in the interim, a case against Mexico appeared to change the rules for determining subsidy. At issue was some $5 billion of trade—the third-largest item in Canada's exports to the United States—which meant the case was treated as high politics in Ottawa.

The U.S. Department of Commerce handed down a preliminary ruling on October 16, 1986, that concluded that timber pricing policies of Canadian provinces constituted subsidies. It imposed a 15 percent preliminary countervailing duty on lumber imports from Canada. The date set for the final ruling was December 30, 1986, leaving the period between October and December for negotiation. The negotiation between the two countries was difficult, leading to speculation that the situation could erupt into an outright trade war.[13] The negotiation within Canada was also difficult. The province of Ontario wanted to see the case through, gambling that the final decision would be in line with the 1983 case that had gone in Canada's favor. British Columbia, however, wanted to raise the price of lumber exports and thereby avoid the U.S. duty, which would keep the money in Canada.

An agreement was reached on December 30, but it did not improve relations between the two countries. Canada agreed to apply an export tax equal to the 15 percent countervailing duty, and on that basis, the lumber companies dropped the countervail suit. However, suspicious that Canadian provincial governments might try to rebate the taxes to the Canadian producers, the U.S. companies insisted that the U.S. government retain the right to monitor the arrangements put in place by Canada. Canada reluctantly accepted this provision.

The softwood lumber countervailing duty case was a profound shock to the Canadian government. In the first place, U.S. trade remedy law appeared to put it in a position to dictate its trading partner's natural resource pricing policies. Canada argued however that it had a comparative advantage in trees, and quite apart from tax policies, economic rationality alone would seem to dictate that the price for standing timber would be lower in Canada than elsewhere. The fact that the United States had forced a price increase on Canadian exports was widely viewed as a bullying tactic.[14] Second, the arrangements put in place to avoid the countervailing duty may have retained the increased taxes in Canada, but they limited Canada's ability to assist lumber companies facing layoffs or closures because of the export tax.[15] This agreement was viewed by many Canadians as an abridgment of Canada's domestic economic sovereignty. It was as if the U.S. government had found itself forced to negotiate a deal with Japan that would prevent an action such as the bailout of the Chrysler Corporation.

The *second stage* of the negotiation, which consisted of seventeen formal bargaining sessions, lasted from mid-November 1986 to the breakdown of talks on September 23, 1987. After an impact study was completed by the U.S. International Trade Commission in January 1987, the two sides had little difficulty negotiating an across-the-board elimination of each other's tariffs. On services, the United States had tabled a comprehensive proposal that would have made the right to "market access" a part of the deal. Market access, or the right to establish in foreign markets, goes well beyond traditional trade law, which usually only specifies the rules that govern exchanges without obliging governments to permit those exchanges in the first place. Canada was decidedly lukewarm about the concept of market access, and some believed that some sectors in the United States would also have difficulty with this proposal.[16]

The Canadian press covered the entire negotiation, generating a notoriety for senior negotiators and promoting debate, particularly on sensitive issues. For example, there was strong opposition in Canada (especially Ontario) to including the auto agreement in the negotiation, and indeed the Canadian government refused repeatedly and symbolically to discuss the subject: "If it ain't broke, don't fix it," Reisman said frequently. However, the Canadians did discuss auto tariffs, which constitute important sanctions within the auto agreement, and the press frequently commented on the place of the auto agreement in the negotiations.[17] Another example was cultural industries. It was well understood that Canada would seek a general exception on cultural industries in any eventual agreement, but the American side sought to limit this exclusion as much as possible. Again the press managed to provoke interest in the possibility of negotiation on the issue, turning it into a source of misunderstanding and possible manipulation throughout the negotiation.

As the negotiation wore on, Canada became increasingly insistent that the United States establish a distinct set of rules to govern Canada-U.S. trade, which would effectively exempt Canadian exports from existing U.S. trade remedies. A related demand was for a binational dispute settlement mechanism that would remove future disputes from exclusive U.S. jurisdiction. Both demands had maximum political visibility in Canada. It was frequently said that the United States pursued a "trade irritants approach" in its negotiation with Canada, but trade irritants had a profound impact on Canadian negotiation strategy as well.[18] The U.S. negotiators rejected outright any possibility of blanket exemption to U.S. trade law for Canada, and in general, they remained noncommittal about negotiating incremental changes in this area while trying to up the ante in other areas that were difficult for Canada, notably energy and investment. Canada resisted adding investment to the agenda until late in the negotiation, and a working group for this issue was first established in May 1987.[19] For a time, the Canadian team tried to link concessions on investment to concessions on dispute settlement, but as the demandeur in the negotiation, Canada eventually found it necessary to put an offer on investment on the table before it had received much on dispute settlement. The role of being the initiator of concessions is a difficult one in negotiation, and it was later colorfully described by Reisman as being asked to "undress while they [the Americans] were sitting there looking you over to see whether they were interested. . . ."[20]

As the negotiation drew to a close, the differences in the political seniority of the two negotiating teams again created problems for the negotiation. Access to senior officials was assured on the Canadian side but not on the American side, thus creating a problem of imbalance that ultimately left the Canadian side unwilling to continue the negotiation. Throughout the negotiation a common Canadian tactic had been to elevate the process to a political level wherever possible. Canada took advantage of summit meetings between President Reagan and Prime Minister Mulroney, as well as the Venice Economic Summit in June 1987 to press its case for dispute settlement and other issues.

The continuing pressure by Canada appeared to pay off when President Reagan's State of the Union address in January 1987 contained a reference to the need to complete "an historic free-trade agreement" between Canada and the United States.[21] This reference appeared to ensure that the talks were on the administration's agenda, but on this point, the signals were mixed. For example, in August, when the talks were most intense, a lengthy *New York Times* summary of the administration priorities based on interviews with senior White House staff failed to even mention the Canada-U.S. trade talks. On the Canadian side, there was a certain sense of inevitability about the problems of attracting high-level attention in Washington.

On September 23, 1987, at the twenty-second meeting of the two negotiating teams, Simon Reisman announced that the United States was "not responding on elements fundamental to Canada's position" and suspended the talks.[22] Much had been accomplished up to that point, including a nearly complete reduction on tariffs, and preliminary drafting of agreements in other areas such as agriculture, services, investment, and energy. However, Canada continued to press the United States for a binding arbitration mechanism that would circumvent U.S. trade remedies, while the United States demanded commitments from Canada on the use of subsidies that went well beyond the standard in existing U.S. trade law. The result was a standoff and a breakdown of the negotiation.

The breakdown came as no surprise. Because of the political visibility of past trade actions, such as on softwood lumber, the Canadian government put increasing emphasis on the "binding" element in a dispute settlement mechanism. Exactly what "binding" meant was not entirely clear, but it was probably best defined by Canadian trade minister Patricia Carney as "something that reduces uncertainty," that is, something that would eliminate the uncertainty of future trade remedy actions against Canadian exporters. At the same time, U.S. leaders from the president on down made it clear that a blanket exception to U.S. trade law was not negotiable. In sum, what Canada had publicly and frequently described as its bottom line was simply unacceptable to the United States.

The *third stage* of the negotiation, which was precipitated by the Canadian walkout, lasted from Wednesday, September 23, to Sunday, October 4. The immediate effect of the walkout was to raise the level of negotiation. Since this had been an objective of Canada for some time it led some Americans to view the Canadian move as being driven more by tactics than by substance. It also led to criticism from some in Congress, who felt less able to control senior administration officials than the trade bureaucrats who had been carrying the negotiation.

On the U.S. side, responsibility for the negotiation was quickly assumed by Treasury Secretary James Baker, who was chairman of the influential Economic Policy Council, and U.S. Trade Representative Clayton Yeutter. In Canada, the negotiation was effectively managed from the prime minister's office, under the direction of Derek Burney, chief of staff. The mood in Canada was mixed, but the government was agreed that the next move was up to the Americans. Perhaps the most negative note came from Reisman himself. In televised interviews, Reisman was sharply critical of U.S. negotiating strategy, declaring, "There was nobody really in charge in the United States."[23]

Treasury Secretary Baker initiated an urgent round of consultations and analyses on September 23. The Americans quickly concluded, first, that an agreement would meet important U.S. objectives, and even more important, a failure would be a damaging blow to the administration. Second, they concluded that there was enough room for maneuvering to make agreement possible; for example, Canada was already demonstrating flexibility in downgrading its rhetoric surrounding the dispute settlement issue from "binding" to "definitive" to "objective and impartial."[24] On Saturday, September 26, Prime Minister Mulroney received a new proposal from the United States, on the basis of which he dispatched Burney, Wilson, and Carney to meet with Baker and Yeutter on Monday.

The United States had already agreed to accept a more or less automatic bilateral dispute settlement process for disputes that arose over the trade rules agreed to in the FTA. Thus the emphasis was on reaching agreement on joint rules governing subsidies, dumping, and so forth. The two sides had reached an impasse on these.

Previous U.S. proposals had contained lists of Canadian subsidies divided into two categories of allowable or objectionable (that is, countervailable).[25] This approach was unacceptable to Canada, which insisted on framing subsidy rules in terms of broad principles that would be applicable to both sides. The new proposal from Baker appeared to move in the direction of general principles, and therefore a lengthy negotiation session was held at the Treasury Department on Monday, September 28, followed by an exchange of telephone calls and proposals on succeeding days. The negotiators were, however, unable to break the deadlock on subsidies, and the negotiation appeared doomed.[26] Then, at mid-week, Baker met with the Senate Finance Committee. In a surprising turn of events spearheaded by Senator Bill Bradley of New Jersey, the committee members subsequently agreed to a different approach to the negotiation. On this basis, Baker called Ottawa on Thursday night, and the parties explored the new U.S. proposal.

The new approach called for both sides to agree to postpone the issue of subsidies until some future date. Meanwhile, the trade remedy legislation in both countries would remain intact. The United States would agree to an ad hoc binational panel review process, but until new rules were established the panels would operate on the basis of each country's domestic antidump and countervail legislation. The main power of the panels would be that of judicial-like review over antidump and countervail cases. Normally, in the United States, this power was exercised first by the Court of International Trade in New York, and on appeal by the Court of Appeals for the Federal Circuit in Washington, D.C. For some in the U.S. government, and particularly for the New York trade bar, this proposal was tantamount to a loss of national sovereignty; there was also a question of whether it would even be constitutional. For Canada, it was equally symbolic, for it represented the last hope of getting a handle on the trade remedy system of the United States.

The new approach provided the basis for a final marathon session in Washington on October 2-3. With both technical and political personnel in attendance, the deal came together very quickly.[27] The focus continued to be dispute settlement, but in key areas such as investment, financial services, culture, and alcoholic beverages both parties exchanged concessions they had been previously withholding until the last minute. With virtually the entire agreement concluded, attention then turned back to the last outstanding issue, the operation of the binational tribunal. It was then Saturday evening, a few hours before the midnight deadline.

The last demand of the Canadians was assurance that Congress would not be able to revoke a decision of the binational tribunal. This demand was not hypothetical, because earlier versions of the Omnibus Trade bill had included provisions that would have altered the basis of the ruling in the 1983 Softwood Lumber case that had gone in Canada's favor. For the Americans, the demand appeared impossible to meet; Congress is constitutionally empowered to regulate foreign commerce, and the agreement with Canada could not bind future Congresses. For the Canadians, however, the demand was a deal-breaker; without it, there was no agreement. At about eight o'clock Saturday night, the Canadians concluded there was no agreement and communicated this to Secretary Baker. Then, according to Trade Minister Carney's account: "Jim Baker . . . got out of his armchair, walked out of his office, went to the lawyers and told them to be creative. That was the moment."[28]

What Baker returned with was a proposal that future amendments to antidump or countervail laws that affected goods from the other country would be required to name that party in the amending legislation. This was a meaningful constraint, since Congress normally is reluctant to identify specific parties as targets of general legislation. Baker also proposed that future statutory amendments be subject to a binational panel that would have the right to review amendments, and to issue declaratory opinions as to whether challenged amendments were consistent with the Agreement. Baker's proposals did not bind Congress or the Canadian Parliament, but in a world of sovereign nations they went a long way to ensure that the interests of the other party were protected in future legislation. Baker's offer was accepted before midnight. It essentially completed the "Elements of the Agreement," and the president and prime minister were so informed.[29]

The *fourth stage* of the negotiation, which went from October 5 to December 11, 1987, entailed turning the "Elements of Agreement" into a complete legal text, based on which both countries could draft implementing legislation. The deadline for the delivery of the text was January 2. Given the documents at issue, the negotiations faced a daunting task. The "Elements" was a 35-page paper that outlined the Agreement. The final text was a formal legal document of some 250 pages, with 21 chapters and numerous annexes. The atmosphere in which the negotiators worked was intense, and both governments were being pressed by constituents to reveal the details of FTA.

The task of drafting the Agreement was coordinated by Charles (Chip) Roh of the USTR and Konrad von Finckenstein of the TNO. Each assigned a team of lawyers to the task, and used work groups to handle specialized areas of the Agreement. Drafts were written, exchanged, and reconciled in a tedious point-by-point, line-by-line process. Clearly, any such extensive drafting process would encounter problems of policy, which required assembling negotiators at intervals during the autumn to hammer out additional understandings. The final such meeting at the political level took place in early December. Decisions were made on outstanding issues, which generally involved the dropping of difficult demands that each side had made of the other. The way was then clear for the Agreement. The negotiation was over.

## Dispute Settlement: The Linchpin of the Negotiation

Complex negotiations often have a linchpin, a main issue that has to be resolved for the negotiation to reach overall agreement. A linchpin issue may or may not be important in substance, but it is by definition important procedurally. Dispute settlement was the linchpin of the FTA. The Canadians who initiated the negotiation decided they could not reach agreement without concluding this issue, and the passage of time simply reinforced that decision. For the Americans, a focus on dispute settlement was simply part of the price of admission to the negotiation. It was a bothersome problem that would not go away.

Why did dispute settlement become so important? Companies and business people—the constituents of trade policy—are usually disinterested in the dispute settlement portions of trade agreements. Lawyers care about dispute settlement, but nevertheless lawyers from both sides who negotiated the FTA felt the issue had been overblown. If the U.S.-Canadian case were compared to the Australian–New Zealand bilateral trade agreement, one striking difference would be the nearly complete absence of formal dispute settlement procedures in the latter agreement. What accounts for the differences? The answer lies in the nature of the two countries and their perceptions of recent trade disputes.

Fair trade—or a "level playing field"—is a long-standing goal of U.S. trade policy. In practice, it means that trade should be conducted by recognized rules, and that government intervention in the marketplace should be kept to a minimum. In the event that foreign producers or their governments violate accepted rules, U.S. law provides remedies for domestic producers who compete with imports. A concept of trade remedies (especially antidump and countervail) is built into the GATT and followed by most trading nations. For example, Canadian antidump and countervail legislation is similar to that of the United States.

Of course, trade remedy legislation becomes most problematic when applied to government subsidies. The legal theory is that, if a foreign government subsidizes a producer, the products exported by that producer represent unfair competition to producers in the importing country if they cause or threaten material injury. Consequently, this creates a right of remedy. The remedy is a countervailing duty that is applied following a determination that the foreign subsidy exists and that it causes material injury to the domestic producer. Until the mid-1970s, the United States did not vigorously pursue countervail suits. However, with the Trade Agreements Act of 1979 (which implemented the Tokyo Round accords), Congress set forth detailed and transparent requirements for the countervail process, provided ample judicial review, and moved the administration of countervail suits from the Department of the Treasury to Commerce. As a result, the countervail process is more accessible, and the number of cases has increased sharply in the 1980s.

Beyond the legal procedures, however, lies a deeper political concern. In order to promote the rights of the individual against society, the United States operates a more litigious system than other countries. In the trade world, this is expressed by unfair trade remedy laws. These laws form a kind of safety valve for protectionist pressures, and without them it is questionable whether any support for trade liberalization would continue to exist in the United States. The safety valve feature of trade remedies is a historic concept, but it is especially important in a period of record trade deficits. It is feared that, if domestic industry did not have the individual right to seek trade remedies, there would be stronger collective pressure for sweeping protectionist legislation.

The Canadian side of this issue is that the United States has used trade remedies excessively, particularly countervailing duties, to the point where they become a form of "contingency protectionism," that is, protection when and where you need it.[30] Canada feels it has bought and paid for access to the U.S. market with its participation in previous GATT negotiations, but this access is directly threatened by trade remedies and, even more important, indirectly threatened by the uncertainty produced by trade remedies. It is argued that trade remedies are mainly a means for U.S. producers to harrass foreign businesses; they give U.S. industries that have lost out in the economic marketplace a chance to win back business from their Canadian competitors through a costly legal procedure conducted entirely within U.S. institutions. The fact that trade remedies appear to have been initiated only after Canadian trade has become well established creates the impression that they are a penalty for being economically successful. Not only is this an emotional issue for Canadian business, it also calls into question the fundamental wisdom of establishing closer trade ties with the United States.

The problem of countervail is logically preceded by subsidy. The view in the United States has been that Canadian governments (federal and provincial) subsidized their producers heavily, which arguably is supported by recent studies such as the Neilsen report.[31] It is argued that American producers should have some recourse against these subsidy practices. Canadian governments do not deny using subsidies; indeed, they are quite open about using these tools to offset regional disparities and to promote economic development in Canada's poorer regions. Ironically, the very openness may contribute to U.S. criticism; if so, the situation would be reminiscent of European criticisms of preferential government procurement policies of the United States, which are prominently displayed as "buy American" provisions in U.S. law rather than existing as more subtle forms of administrative directives. In its defense, Canada has argued that it uses subsidies mainly to offset the infrastructural weaknesses of a small economy, and that this use is not a significant factor in international trade.[32] Furthermore, it has contended that some of the practices U.S. industry objected to did not constitute subsidies at all, such as the natural resource pricing practices of provincial governments that figured prominently in the softwood lumber dispute.

One of Canada's principal objectives in the free trade negotiation was to secure its access to the U.S. market, that is, to reduce the impact of U.S. trade remedies, especially countervailing duties on Canadian products, either directly by negotiating an exception to U.S. trade law, or indirectly by creating a dispute settlement system that would circumvent those laws. During the negotiation, security of access (or dispute settlement, which it boiled down to) became the paramount objective of the Canadian side because it was the one area where Canada was unquestionably the demandeur and thus in a position to "get something" from the negotiation. On many other issues, and certainly on tariffs, investment, financial services, automotive, and services, Canada was arguably in a position where it would have to give more than it got. Dispute settlement was thus necessary to help sell the agreement in Canada. Moreover, it was a politically visible issue, and it was one easily understood by politicians and constituents who ordinarily paid little attention to trade policy.

Dispute settlement also became important because of the negotiating environment. The aforementioned shakes and shingles and softwood lumber cases occurred during the free trade negotiation, and dramatically focused attention in Canada on the need for a different arrangement with the United States. At the same time, the progress of the Omnibus Trade bill in the U.S. Congress, which in its early stages was sharply protectionist, worried the Canadian government. In particular, it worried about proposed changes that would make countervail procedures even more accessible to U.S. industry, reinforcing fears that the future might bring increased use of trade remedies by the United States, with a consequent increase in economic uncertainty for Canadian business.

Finally, dispute settlement became paramount because Canada's trade negotiator, presumably backed by the prime minister, made it so. The issue appeared to be a concern of the TNO and not wholly a response to constituency pressure. What generated it was the notion that Canada was seeking to negotiate "national treatment" with the United States, within which the concept of unfair trade remedy was simply inappropriate. Dispute settlement was seen as a means to create a new, economically rational relationship with the United States, one that would effectively remove the national border for the purpose of economic exchange.

The negotiating strategy pursued by Canada on trade remedies was to focus on the practice and not on the remedy. The theory was that if Canada and the United States could reach agreement on the practice—for example, on permissible versus impermissible subsidies—then countervail would by definition no longer be needed, and Canada could be wholly exempted from U.S. countervail legislation. Although sound in concept, this proposal did not make for effective communication between the two sides. U.S. negotiators doubted Canada's willingness to curb subsidy practices, and saw the proposal as a means for Canada to escape U.S. trade remedies. There was strong resistance in the Department of Commerce (which administers countervail legislation) to even negotiate trade remedies with Canada at all, and sensitivities were so high among some congressmen that U.S. negotiators resisted establishing a work group until after January 1987.

Once the negotiation was joined, extreme proposals from both sides dominated the exchanges, and the negotiation went nowhere. To the Americans, the Canadians appeared to be backing themselves into a corner by making an irreduceable demand that everyone from the president on down had said was a nonstarter. Indeed, in all probability, it was the futility of negotiating an exception to U.S. trade remedy law, which had been previously demonstrated in the U.S.-Israel free trade agreement,[33] that contributed to the U.S. inaction and Canadian charges that the United States was unprepared for the negotiation. To the Canadians, the Americans appeared completely unwilling to address any mechanism, such as a subsidies code, that might mitigate the impact of trade remedies on Canada. Throughout the summer the attention remained focused on subsidies. Finally, pressed by the Canadians, the Americans made their first complete proposal in August 1987. As viewed from the Canadian side, the proposal was extreme; as one negotiator put it, "The proposal would have taken all Canadian governments out of the subsidy business altogether." The proposal was rejected by Canada.

The United States proposed a second text in September, which was known colloquially as the "safe harbors" text. It contained a list of Canadian subsidy practices, with a line across the page differentiating those practices which were countervailable from those that were not (hence the safe harbor). The text led to a serious but ultimately unprofitable exchange on the meaning of subsidy. One problem was regional development. Regional development is a constitutional issue in Canada, and as a concept it receives widespread support in the Canadian population and among Canadian governments, federal and provincial. The have-not provinces in Canada take a hard line on this issue: for example, during the negotiation, the four Atlantic provinces transmitted a document to Ottawa proposing that any province falling below 85 percent of the average national wealth be completely free of any disciplines on subsidies under a free trade agreement. This proposal is admittedly extreme, but it reflects a commonly held Canadian view that government has an obligation to redress economic disparities between Canada's different regions. There is no equivalent viewpoint in the United States. From the perspective of U.S. trade policy, it is clear that the Atlantic provinces proposal would be completely outside current U.S. practice, which takes account of the nature of a subsidy and not the nature of the recipient of the subsidy in determining whether a subsidy is permissible or countervailable. Thus regional development is one area where differing national practices and differing philosophies of government make it difficult to work out common rules on trade.

Another problem with the subsidy negotiation was that the United States was unwilling to negotiate in terms of general principles, or to accept that such disciplines negotiated with Canada would also apply to U.S. practices. The fact that U.S. governments—state and federal—make use of subsidies has been documented,[34] and U.S. negotiators are prepared to admit that fact. Furthermore, most subsidies are given by state governments, and are not under the control of Washington. As an experienced U.S. trade lawyer remarked in Canada:

> The countries are very different, but the general tone of government assistance in the two countries is not all that different. . . our subsidies are through the states. That's why the United States couldn't bind them.[35]

U.S. trade law does not define subsidy, and it became apparent that in the negotiation with Canada, U.S. negotiators were not prepared to define it either. For the Americans, the main issue was the impact of a subsidy practice on trade, and if that impact was harmful, the practice should be met with a remedy. However, Canadians wanted an objective definition of what constituted permissible practices, and they assumed that such definition would apply to the U.S. government as well as to Canada. Clearly, this produced an impasse, because if parties are unable to define a practice, neither will they be able to regulate it.

The reason why the United States was unable to negotiate a definition of subsidy is a matter of size and ideology. Because of the difference in size between Canada and the United States, and the resulting different proportion of bilateral trade in the economy of both countries, almost any major subsidy program initiated in Canada is likely through trade to have an affect on the United States, whereas equivalent subsidy programs in the United States would be unlikely to affect Canada. In Canada, the incentive for governments to accept disciplines on subsidies is the prospect of being free of retaliation of U.S. countervail: this is not true in the United States. Thus a difference in size creates a difference in the impact of trade—and that makes negotiation of common rules problematic.

But that is not all. In trade, the United States is much more affected by third parties than is Canada. Were the United States to reach agreement with Canada on the definition and principles of subsidy practices, such an agreement would be used as a starting point by America's trade partners in any subsequent negotiation. This could constitute, in the view of U.S. negotiators, "unilateral disarmament" vis-a-vis the European Community and other parties whose subsidy practices are more worrisome to the United States than Canada's. In sum, the difference in size between Canada and the United States created an inherent imbalance in the talks on subsidies, and rendered the situation exceedingly difficult to negotiate.

Finally, ideology and attitudes played a role in the negotiation. Canada's approach to subsidy is that it is a legitimate tool of government, and by the end of the negotiation, the Canadian delegation was prepared to accept—on a reciprocal basis—meaningful constraints on the use of this tool. By comparison, the United States has a history of viewing subsidies as unacceptable, a viewpoint well represented in the business community and Congress. And it is a viewpoint that makes trade bureaucrats very nervous about reaching agreements with foreign countries that distinguish permissible from impermissible subsidies. In effect, Canada was pressing the United States toward a fundamental shift in attitude toward trade and industrial policy, and the free trade negotiation did not provide enough time or incentive for that shift to occur.

As long as both sides focused on subsidies, they were engaged in trying to force the other side to approve their own domestic practices—a futile endeavor. It may have been logical to lead the discussion with the measures and not remedies (that is, subsidy and not countervail), but it was not political. In terms of trade diplomacy, the problem had always been the U.S. use of trade remedies. The agreement succeeded when the discussion shifted from subsidies to trade remedies, and when both sides recognized that something could be salvaged on dispute settlement without having to agree on subsidies. What was salvaged assured that Canadians had a hand on the wheel in any future U.S. actions against Canada. This assurance went a considerable distance toward meeting the Canadian government's goal of reducing the uncertainty faced by Canadian producers in exporting to the United States.

The combination that unlocked the negotiation, that is, the replacement of judicial review by a binational panel, came initially from Congress. It was the brainchild of Sam Gibbons, chairman of the House Ways and Means Trade Subcommittee, and it hung in the air about a week or so until Canadian Ambassador Alan Gotlieb and others realized its potential. The interesting point is that the idea came from Congress, which from the Canadian perspective had always appeared to be the main enemy on dispute settlement. Even more interesting is that the Senate Finance Committee, once the prospect for an outright exemption to trade remedy legislation was dropped, proved remarkably docile in light of the real constraints that were negotiated to U.S. countervail procedures. At the eleventh hour, the real pressure on the American side came from within the U.S. bureaucracy, and especially from the International Trade Administration of the Department of Commerce, the body responsible for administering countervail procedures.

In the end, the real constituents of U.S. trade remedies were not so much Congress, which makes the law, or business, which profits from the law, but rather government lawyers whose jobs are to enforce the law. The dispute settlement negotiation demonstrated that changes in economic policies demanded by trading partners are often most problematic for the government officers who administer those policies, and that much of what is called protectionism "is a bureaucratic conception of how the national economy should be managed and how it should relate to the international economy."[36] This phenomenon occurs frequently in trade negotiations, and there were other examples of it—such as the defense of subsidy practices by Canadian federal and provincial bureaucrats—in the Canada-U.S. negotiation.

# Chapter 4
# Results of the Agreement

The Canada-U.S. free trade agreement is a comprehensive agreement that covers tariffs, nontariff barriers (NTBs), and institutional arrangements. It liberalizes trade between the United States and Canada, and it increases the stability of the political environment within which trade and investment are conducted between the two countries. The FTA includes a separate chapter on investment, but in a sense the whole agreement is about investment. In the modern world economy, trade and investment are complementary. Particularly on the Canadian side, it was recognized that Canada's economy could not become more competitive without access to investment (both foreign *and* Canadian), and that new investment could not be mobilized unless Canada had assured access to a market larger than its own. These concerns stimulated the Canadian government to press for the most comprehensive agreement possible with the United States; the United States also favored a comprehensive agreement because that would help it achieve its economic policy goals.

The FTA was negotiated pursuant to GATT Article XXIV, which provides for the establishment of free trade associations among Contracting Parties. The FTA was consistent with and drew on the GATT, but in many areas it went well beyond trade agreements that have been negotiated under GATT auspices. The FTA can be viewed as a mixture of old issues and new issues, that is, issues that have previously been featured in GATT or North American trade agreements versus issues that are novel in the context of trade negotiation. Under old issues would be included dispute settlement, which is a traditional GATT issue on which novel arrangements were negotiated in the FTA; tariffs; government procurement; technical barriers to trade (or standards); agriculture, including trade in alcoholic beverages; and automotive products. Under new issues would be included services, investment, financial services, and energy.[1] This listing includes the major items in the FTA, although there were a number of miscellaneous provisions that dealt with specific trade irritants or provided rules for interpreting the overall agreement.

### Dispute Settlement

The dispute settlement provisions of the FTA are covered in two chapters. In Chapter 18 of the Agreement, all disputes (except those dealing with financial services or arising under antidump or countervail laws) are subject to a process that includes notification, provision of information, consultation, referral to a joint commission, and finally arbitration. Some of these procedures, such as notification or consultation, are adopted from existing GATT practices; others, such as the establishment of a joint commission or binding arbitration, are novel to the Canada-U.S. FTA. In Chapter 19 of the Agreement, the parties are committed to three main undertakings: the establishment, through subsequent negotiation, of joint rules surrounding subsidy and dumping; bilateral review of any changes either party makes to existing antidump and countervail laws; and the establishment of binational panels to replace internal judicial review on countervail and antidump actions. These rules represent an advance over those negotiated in the subsidies code at the Tokyo Round.

The issue of "binding" dispute settlement was critical for Ottawa, and it was the occasion for much hype in the political process during the negotiation. "Binding" came to be interpreted in Canada to mean that national trade laws such as countervail would be submitted to compulsory arbitration by impartial external bodies, which in turn would have authority to nullify those laws that unfairly threatened Canadian exporters. Clearly, this goal was not achieved in the FTA, which reaffirms the right of each party to apply its own antidump and countervail laws pending the creation of new trade rules in subsequent negotiation. This apparent weakness of the FTA dispute settlement procedure has drawn much criticism in Canada; however, there are areas where the Agreement provides for binding actions, which incidentally are more likely to work to the advantage of the smaller party.

The FTA establishes binding procedures in three areas. The first area is safeguards (that is, emergency or escape clause actions pursuant to Article XIX of the GATT). The FTA specifies that, in the event consultations are unsuccessful, disputes over emergency actions shall be taken to binding arbitration on such terms as the commission may adopt. This is an extraordinary power, and as noted by Canadian trade lawyer Debra Steger: "The ability of an international panel to review and make binding decisions concerning a country's use of safeguards measures under Article XIX of the GATT is without precedent in any international agreement."[2] This procedure might have been very important to Canada in the shakes and shingles case.

A second area of binding authority occurs in binational panel reviews, which replaced judicial review (for example, by the U.S. Court of International Trade) of antidump or countervail cases. The role of the binational panels is to ensure that any antidumping duties or countervailing duties that have been awarded have been fairly determined according to the trade laws of the respective parties. This procedure does not permit exporters to avoid the trade laws in the country of import, but it does act as a reasonable guarantee that those laws will not be abused. To Canadians, U.S. trade law procedures are held to have become politicized to the detriment of Canadian exporters; for example, Canadian analysts Alan Rugman and Andrew Anderson have stated that U.S. trade law "is in a state of virtual anarchy," and that "U.S. trade law is not administered in a manner consistent with the GATT subsidies code."[3] The binational panel review process should be able to deal effectively and fairly with these Canadian accusations.

A third area of binding dispute settlement includes all disputes mutually agreed by the parties (Article 1806). It provides for the possibility of enlarging the scope of binding dispute settlement in the future, which is a distinct possibility if the FTA proves to be a durable arrangement.

Contained in the FTA are also procedures for writing new trade laws on antidump and countervail. These procedures have set a deadline of seven years for the development of new rules, after which either party could terminate the FTA on six months' notice. It is difficult to predict how important these procedures and deadline will be to the FTA. U.S. commentators have regularly claimed that antidump and countervail only affect a very small proportion of total Canada-U.S. trade, and it is possible that if U.S. trade balances improve in the future, U.S. industries may be less concerned about competing imports.[4] If that is the case, the whole issue may fade away. On the other hand, it is undeniable that recent actions (particularly on soft wood lumber) have raised the countervail issue to enormous proportions in Canadian politics, and further actions of this sort would undoubtedly increase the pressure in Canada to back out of the Agreement. The safest political judgment at the present time is that new rules for antidump and countervail are urgently needed in the Canada-U.S. economic relationship, and the FTA structures are the best, and perhaps only, prospect for negotiating such new rules.

For the immediate future, the United States and Canada would be well off to work within the FTA system, which resolves some but not all of the uncertainty surrounding the countervail process. One question that immediately arises is whether the FTA system would have made any difference in the second softwood lumber case. Given the case was resolved by negotiation prior to a final award of countervailing duties, any answer must be conjectural. Furthermore, the case occurred during a period when U.S. law on countervail was in flux, which makes generalization from this situation even more difficult.

In the event of another countervailing duty case, Canada may be far less inclined to negotiate; it might choose to see the countervail procedure through to a conclusion and then resort to binational review if it felt it had a case. In itself, this would likely deter frivolous cases from being initiated by U.S. producers. If the matter then went to binational review, Canadian lawyers would be involved and the panel would have access to the entire administrative record of the case. Such a procedure would offer reasonable assurance that the panel could resolve any accusations that the procedure was politicized or not administered in accordance with national and international law. As a result, the appearance of objectivity would be increased, and the likelihood that a legal disagreement could become a political and diplomatic disagreement as well would be lessened.

### Tariffs

The tariff agreement is the most significant part of the FTA from the standpoint of trade liberalization, but it received relatively little public attention. It is an example of that which is most important economically being least controversial politically. Tariff reductions constitute tax reductions, and they represent price changes to business and consumers. Tariff reductions have a real and direct effect on trade, in comparison to a legal code that might be important but whose benefits might be indirect. With tariff reductions, business people can calculate the change in their market position and economists can project aggregate effects of the change.

The FTA completely eliminated all tariffs between Canada and the United States, without exception, over a ten-year period. Tariffs in some sectors will be removed when the Agreement enters into force on January 1, 1989. For other sectors, tariff reductions will be phased in over five annual increments, or ten annual increments, depending on the time needed for the sector to adjust. In addition to tariffs, various other customs matters were cleared up between the two countries. For example, both parties agreed to eliminate duty drawbacks (that is, a refund of duties on products such as components that are exported after being imported) on third-party goods so that they will not undercut bilateral preferences; and the United States agreed to eliminate a customs user fee (currently 0.17 percent) on goods coming from Canada.

The United States and Canada will each retain its own multilateral most favored nation (MFN) tariff schedule vis-a-vis all other countries. The retention of individual tariffs on goods coming from third parties is an essential feature of a free trade association, in comparison to a customs union such as the European Community where the parties establish a common external tariff. This point is often misunderstood by the public, and it is occasionally wrongly assumed that the elimination of tariffs will open up the Canadian and American marketplace to competition from Europe, Japan, and the developing countries. Instead, normal duties will continue to be applied to goods from third parties. On goods crossing the Canada-U.S. border, rules of origin will be applied to protect against trans-shipment of goods from a third party into either Canada or the United States and then on to the other FTA member's market. The management of rules of origin is an important function in a free trade association, but it is far less intrusive than the collection of duties, however small. One of the goals of the free trade negotiation that was largely accomplished was the reduction of the role of customs officers at the Canada-U.S. border. As Simon Reisman put it:

> By 1998, most businessmen will regard him [the customs official] as that friendly fellow interested in his rule of origin certificate. No more hassling about duties, valuation, technical regulations, and the like.[5]

The results of the Agreement have been assessed in several different models. The results differ, depending on the assumptions used, but generally they show an increase in trade and production resulting from the FTA. For example, Jeffrey Schott, a U.S. trade analyst, has claimed that, once all tariff cuts are implemented, U.S. exports to Canada should increase by about $2.4 billion while Canadian exports would increase by about $1.1 billion.[6] This assessment is deliberately understated, and includes, for example, only increases in products already traded. An assessment by the Economic Council of Canada was much higher, and predicted two-way trade increasing by nearly $15 billion by 1995; however, this assessment assumed a much larger agreement on government procurement than eventually materialized.[7] Although the amount of increase projected is different, the analyses in both countries show an increased volume of trade resulting from the reduction of tariffs. Employment presents a similar picture. Employment growth in the United States is estimated to be about 32,000 jobs, while estimates of net employment growth in Canada range from 120,000 by the Canadian Department of Finance to 350,000 by the Economic Council.[8] Finally, productivity increases from free trade calculated for Canada generally range from 4 to 10 percent of GNP.[9]

For the United States, the FTA will produce straightforward gains from increased trade. For Canada, however, as noted by Jenness: "The stimulus imparted by trade liberalization will almost all be internally generated."[10] This will be the result because many Canadian plants are suboptimal and produce largely for the small Canadian market. Producing for the larger North American economic system will induce specialization, thereby creating economies of scale and increased productivity. In addition, domestic spending will increase as a result of lower prices due to reduced tariffs. The notion that Canada will realize its largest gain from the reduction of its own tariff has received some support from economists; for example, John Whalley has said that "we may actually get more gain in the long run from eliminating our own barriers than from having U.S. barriers eliminated."[11] Such assertions confirm the aforementioned strategy of the Mulroney government in seeking to use a free trade negotiation as a means to improve the competitiveness and productivity of the Canadian economy.

In economic terms, the tariff arrangement was probably the most important part of the FTA, especially for Canada, but it could not have been negotiated alone. For the United States, the services sector and the various trade irritants were a more compelling reason to negotiate freer trade; for Canada, tariffs presented an unbalanced situation, and it was necessary to bring other elements into the negotiation to redress the balance. Traditionally, tariffs have been negotiated in the GATT from a mercantilist perspective and on the basis of reciprocity. Negotiators have assumed that a tariff reduced is a concession given to another party, and they have carefully calculated reciprocity in tariff bargaining through the use of quantitative measures such as the amount of the tariff revenue forgone from tariff cuts. Had Canada pursued this approach, it probably would have been unable to reach a reciprocal agreement with the United States because its tariffs were much higher on average and covered a larger volume of trade. Instead, Canada took the more economically imaginative approach of viewing tariffs as an impediment to the domestic economy, and it pressed for abolition of tariffs on both sides. In this strategy, Canada found the United States to be a willing partner.

## Technical Barriers and Government Procurement

The FTA included chapters on technical barriers to trade (or standards) and government procurement. In both these areas, multilateral GATT codes were already in existence as a result of the Tokyo Round, which provided a framework for structuring agreement. The FTA reaffirmed the parties' obligations under the GATT codes and made marginal improvements in their operation.

The purpose of the standards code was to ensure that technical regulations such as labeling, packaging requirements, and certifications of product worthiness would not be used to create unnecessary barriers to trade. To this end, the GATT code obliged parties to exchange information on standards and to avoid adopting regulations that could be used as a subtle form of trade discrimination. For example, parties were expected to frame product standards in terms of general performance characteristics instead of characteristics based on particular design or nation-specific attributes. The FTA carried this process further by requiring the parties to take actions like increasing the compatibility of their procedures for approving products, and to refrain from requiring certification bodies to be located within their territories. The standards chapter does not require either party to forgo setting regulations that are needed for health, safety, or social reasons, but it does require that those regulations be applied to foreign and domestic products alike. Specifically, the FTA does not preclude Canada from requiring bilingual labeling of goods, if this is expected of domestic goods as well as imported products.

One standards problem was given special treatment in the FTA, and demonstrated not only the nature of standards but also the process of dispute settlement. The Canada Mortgage and Housing Corporation (CMHC) has refused to authorize the use of C-D grade plywood (a U.S. standard) in houses it finances on the grounds that the product is unable to withstand Canadian winters. American plywood manufacturers wholeheartedly disagree. The FTA called for a further examination of this issue by the CMHC, and then provided for an international panel of experts to review the case if parties were still aggrieved. The CMHC has subsequently reaffirmed its position, and the panel is obliged to report its findings before January 1, 1989. In the event the panel finds for the Americans and the CMHC, an independent body, is still unwilling to alter its ruling, the FTA authorizes the United States to delay the tariff reductions it has agreed to on Canadian plywood products. This case points out a common problem in the standards area, namely, that governments seeking to liberalize trade often can undertake no more than "best efforts" when dealing with certifying bodies that are private or possess independent statutory authority.

The GATT code on government procurement was designed to permit producers to sell goods to foreign governments, an economic opportunity that hitherto was reserved for domestic firms. The code obliged signatories to extend national treatment to products and supplies covered under the agreement, and it provided for more open tendering procedures than had been practiced previously for government contracts. The code applied to contracts valued at over US$171,000, and it covered the purchasing by those entities (that is, government agencies) or portions of entities that signatories placed under the code.

At various points in the negotiation on government procurement, both the United States and Canada explored the possibility of including a comprehensive procurement agreement in the FTA. Such an agreement was especially sought by Canada. The U.S. government procurement market is vast, and opening it up would enormously increase opportunities for Canadian business. Furthermore, preferential procurement practices in the United States have had a harmful effect on Canadian investment patterns; for example, the rail car manufacturer Bombardier has been obliged to locate production in the United States in order to comply with "Buy America" legislation in connection with sales of subway components to the City of New York. In any event, a comprehensive agreement could not be reached. U.S. negotiators determined that a general removal of restrictions—federal, state, and provincial—would have been unbalanced due to the 10:1 ratio between the procurement markets in the United States and Canada. This decision may have been politically advantageous for both countries, for it avoided the complication of negotiating new procurement rules with state and provincial governments.

The government procurement chapter of the FTA lowered the threshold of the contract value for goods covered by the GATT code from US$171,000 to US$25,000, which is expected to increase the procurement market in Canada by about $500 million and in the United States by about $3 billion. By comparison, the original Tokyo Round code opened up about $12.5 billion of federal government purchasing in the United States, out of a possible $50 billion market in 1979. The FTA also made improvements in the direction of greater transparency in bidding procedures. In sum, the parties did not make much progress on government procurement, which is a disappointment, given that they were working in an area where the ground had already been broken. Any further progress will now have to be accomplished at the multilateral Uruguay Round of the GATT.

### Automotive Products

The trade between the United States and Canada in automotive products is massive, constituting about one-third of bilateral merchandise trade. This trade is covered by the Automotive Products Trade Agreement of 1965 (the Auto Pact), which continues to be the basic automotive trade policy structure between the two countries. All the FTA did in this area was clear up a number of ancillary problems that have arisen in bilateral auto trade over recent years, but it does indirectly affect some operating aspects of the Auto Pact.

The Auto Pact was established in a period of crisis in the Canadian auto industry, which mainly consisted of subsidaries of U.S. automakers. Until 1965, the Canadian industry operated behind high tariff walls and lacked a market of sufficient size to achieve efficient production. To stimulate productivity, the Canadian government offered a duty remission program whereby auto firms were rebated duties paid on imports, based on increased exports. This scheme was effectively an export subsidy, and a countervail suit was launched by a U.S. auto parts manufacturer. To head off the countervail suit, the United States and Canada negotiated the Auto Pact. The Auto Pact provided for tariff-free trade in autos and original parts, accompanied by investment safeguards for the Canadian industry. Specifically, Canada limited duty-free access to qualifying automakers, that is, firms that produced roughly as many cars in Canada as they sold in Canada. Also, firms were to get 60 percent Canadian content in cars sold in Canada. The pact improved the industry's efficiency, and the safeguards stimulated a large round of investment in Canada in the late 1960s. Auto trade increased enormously between the United States and Canada. Today, although Canadian firms operate well beyond the production levels required by the safeguards, government, industry, and labor strongly support the retention of the safeguards as a hedge against economic downturn. This support constrained the Canadian government from negotiating major changes to the pact, despite continued pressure from the U.S. government for removal of the safeguards.

Canada reinstated the duty remission program in 1978 for Volkswagen, despite vigorous U.S. objections. In 1980, programs were offered to Japanese firms, but duties were remitted only for exports to countries other than the United States. Canada dropped this U.S. exclusion in 1984. The effect of the duty remission programs has been to allow foreign firms to import auto parts duty free to Canada in return for increased exports to the United States. The duty remission programs act as export sub-sidies and exacerbate the trade deficit of the United States. The rationale for the program is that Canada is a smaller economy and not as attrac-tive to overseas investors as the United States; duty remissions are a way to ensure that Canada receives its share of international automotive investment. This rationale was undercut, however, by Canada's substantial trade surplus with the United States on auto products.

The automotive goods chapter of the FTA deals with a series of issues generated by the Auto Pact and by various other government trade prac-tices. Most important was duty remission, on which Canada and the United States were on a collision course. As U.S. economist Paul Won-nacott has noted, a countervail suit was becoming more likely in the U.S. auto industry if corrective action was not taken.[12] The FTA eliminated Canada's duty remission programs based on exports to the United States and phased out the production-based remission programs by 1995. Production-based schemes required auto companies to purchase Canadian content, but they did not necessitate an increase in exports. Other features of the FTA included an undertaking that Canada will not add other overseas manufacturers to the list of qualifying manufacturers under the Auto Pact, and an agreement that 50 percent North American content be required for vehicles qualifying for duty-free treatment. The former issue was similar to duty remission, and the United States op-posed adding new manufacturers to the Auto Pact on the grounds that it would stimulate exports into the United States in return for duty-free imports into Canada. The latter issue was hotly contested between the automakers and the parts industry. Parts manufacturers on both sides of the border pressed for a 60 percent content rule, with no success.

### Agriculture and Alcoholic Beverages

The FTA produced some liberalization in agricultural trade, but fell far short of being a major agreement. Both the United States and Canada are net exporters to the world in agriculture, and neither party was prepared to reduce its own agricultural protectionism in view of the much greater protectionism in Europe, Japan, and elsewhere. The FTA did not deal with the sticky issue of agricultural subsidies, largely at U.S. insistence, and it did not affect either country's supply management policies, such as marketing boards in Canada. Even so, the Agreement achieved enough that it may stimulate progress in the area of agricultural protectionism at future multilateral talks.

What the Agreement did do was eliminate all tariffs on agricultural products over the next ten years, but it included a provision that allows Canada to reimpose tariffs temporarily on fresh fruits and vegetables in the event of depressed price conditions. Tariffs are not the main instrument of agricultural protection; nevertheless, the tariff deal is a significant step in the long process of opening up agricultural trade. The aggregate effects of the tariff agreement are hard to determine because of the enormous variety between different products and regions, but U.S. fruit producers are likely to benefit, as well as producers of storable vegetables in eastern Canada. Canadian producers of beef and veal will benefit from a general removal of restrictions on meat imports, while U.S. exporters of chicken will gain from a slight increase in the Canadian quota. On wheat, barley, and oats, Canada agreed to eliminate import licenses when U.S. grain supports become equal to Canadian levels of support. The FTA provides a formula called a producer subsidy equivalent (PSE) to measure the price supports in both countries. This formula is a methodological breakthrough, and could be a point of departure in future multilateral agricultural negotiations held in the GATT.

An important feature of the agricultural sector was Canada's decision to end discriminatory pricing of U.S. wines and spirits. Sales of alcoholic beverages are controlled by provincial liquor boards in Canada, which have followed long-standing policies of applying higher price markups to imported products than those produced locally. The purpose of this policy in all provinces has been to generate revenue, but in provinces where a local wine industry existed, such as Ontario, British Columbia, and Nova Scotia, the policy also provided substantial protection. Canada's trade partners had tried to dismantle this practice before, and as part of the Tokyo Round agreements, Canada provided a "provincial statement of intent" to the European Community (EC) that gave assurances that discriminatory pricing would be curtailed. In fact, the protection was not curtailed, and in some cases the discrimination increased since 1979. To its trade partners, the government of Canada claimed it had limited authority over the situation, since liquor boards were under provincial jurisdiction.

In response to strong pressure from the United States, especially the U.S. wine industry, Canada agreed to end discriminatory pricing on spirits and wine, but no action was taken on beer. The federal government claimed it had constitutional authority under its commercial powers to make the agreement, and it has called upon provincial governments to carry out the action. Meanwhile, in an independent action, the EC initiated a judicial trade action (that is, a GATT panel) against Canada over its pricing practices on alcoholic beverages. The panel found that Canadian provincial liquor boards discriminate against European products, and that the government of Canada has not taken all "reasonable measures" to end the discrimination. The panel report was accepted by the GATT Council in January 1988, and it gave Canada until the end of the year to indicate what measures it would take to remove the discrimination. Interestingly, the defense Canada used against the EC is that it lacks constitutional powers to enforce compliance by the provinces, but that argument seems to be undercut by its position with respect to the FTA.

The GATT liquor board panel underscores the value of the FTA to Canada, for without the Agreement it is likely the United States would have joined the EC action and thereby increased the risk of retaliation to Canada. Nevertheless, the Canadian government is still in a difficult position. Ontario is the most important province in this matter, and it has publicly taken the position that it will not implement the FTA. If it does not do so, Canada would be in a position of noncompliance with the FTA, and more seriously, the GATT Council could authorize the EC to retaliate against Canadian exports. Such retaliation is uncommon, and the most recent case occurred in 1952. However, interest in panels, legal action, and enforcement of legal action has recently picked up in the GATT, as evidenced by the fact that the EC is now preparing a case for retaliation against the United States in connection with a discriminatory environmental tax on petroleum products. It is probable the EC would seek retaliation if Canada were unable to comply with the liquor board panel recommendation, or it is possible that individual member states of the EC might take retaliatory action against Canadian products. The advantage of the latter action is that it would provide a certain symmetry of response against Canada, where the offenders are provinces of, but not, the GATT member.

The liquor case is typical of the problems modern trade policy can create in federal systems. Traditional trade policy mainly involved border measures such as tariffs and quotas, and these were indisputably under the control of national governments. Today, trade policy has expanded to encroach on the tax, regulatory, and procurement policies of governments, and these powers are more likely to be shared between national and subordinate governments. Resolving the problems of divided jurisdiction can be painful. For example, in the liquor board case the Canadian government probably has the authority to prevent provincial governments from importing alcoholic beverages at all, and it has the authority to conduct retail operations itself (at nondiscriminatory prices) through federal mail order outlets. Such an action would meet Canada's overseas obligations to remove discrimination, but it would result in lost sales for exporters and reduced tax revenues for provincial governments. As in so many other trade policy issues, the resolution of the liquor board case is likely to be an awkward compromise among a number of contending parties.

## Services

The FTA broke new ground in international trade negotiation by including services in the Agreement, and none too soon. From the standpoint of economics, trade in services is increasingly mingled with trade in goods, and any trade agreements that did not deal with services would have to be, by definition, limited. Services are obviously critical to the sale, distribution, and maintenance of traded products, and they are of growing importance in the production process as well. From the political standpoint, negotiating services as part of the FTA was inevitable because the United States insisted on its inclusion from the outset. The United States ran a surplus in services with Canada of $1.7 billion in 1985 and $2.3 in 1986, which put it in the position to be a demandeur in this sector.[13] Moreover, U.S. negotiators believed a strong domestic constituency existed for a services deal, and therefore an agreement on services was seen from the earliest moment as necessary to sell the bilateral negotiation in Washington. The fact that services has figured prominently in U.S. strategy in the current GATT negotiation also made it imperative to include services in the negotiation with Canada.

The negotiation took two directions. It was agreed that the first step was to negotiate a code of general rules to govern services trade. Negotiators recognized that, unlike trade in goods, trade in services often requires the establishment of foreign subsidaries to perform service contracts. It followed that one basic rule would be national treatment, which meant that once established in a domestic market foreign firms must be treated no less favorably than domestic firms. Most emphatically this did not mean that governments were unable to regulate the conduct of service industries in the domestic market; rather, it meant that any regulations set down would apply equally to domestic and foreign firms. Another general rule was right of establishment. The United States had previously experienced a problem on this matter with South Korea: the Koreans had extended the principle of national treatment to U.S. insurance firms already in the market but then refused to license new entrants into the domestic market. This action underscored the need to make national treatment and market access complementary goals in establishing service trade, and made it clear that they should form the staple of any negotiation on services.

The second step in negotiating services is to create specific rules for specific sectors of service activity. Specificity is necessary because services are more differentiated than goods. The most common means of extending protectionism on goods have been border measures like the tariff, which can be applied across the board and negotiated generally through the use of devices like tariff-cutting formulas (for example, the elimination of all tariffs is such a formula). Protection on services usually takes the form of industry-specific government regulation; therefore, negotiating services requires establishing a general code of conduct, followed up by specific rules in designated service sectors.

The services chapter of the FTA was pathbreaking by its very existence, but in fact did very little toward liberalizing existing trade in services between Canada and the United States. In Article 1402:5, the Agreement stated that the provisions on services did not apply to nonconforming existing measures, which means that the FTA effectively grandfathered (that is, incorporated from previous statutes) any discrimination now present in Canadian and U.S. government regulations. However, for all new legislation, it provided important disciplines to ensure that trade in services would not become even more restrictive.

Specifically, the FTA identified some sixty-three subcategories of service industries and obliged both parties to treat "persons" (that is, firms) of the other party in the subcategories no less favorably than it treated its own. Elsewhere in the Agreement (under investment, Article 1602), the FTA called on each party to extend national treatment with respect to new business enterprises. These two provisions ensure that new government regulation in the United States and Canada will be consistent with free trade in services. Two other provisions gave further support to nondiscriminatory treatment: one specified that firms of one party may not be arbitrarily obliged to establish a commercial presence in the other;

and the second affirmed that the licensing and certification of individuals to perform services should be related principally to competence. Again, nothing in the Agreement prevented governments from regulating services; they are prevented from regulating discriminatorily on the basis of nationality.

The FTA included three annexes that further define the principles of national treatment and right of access in three service sectors. An annex on architecture dealt with certification and licensing; one on tourism focused on maintenance of agents and rights of promotion; and an annex on computer services and telecommunications prescribed behavior for government monopolies. Finally, the FTA included an important chapter on government immigration regulations respecting temporary entry of business people. The issue of immigration was raised by the Canadian side following the recognition that the most practical problem Canadians faced in providing services in the United States was delays in entering the country due to immigration regulation. The FTA provided for a liberalization of these regulations by both countries.

The services negotiation of the FTA was a concrete step forward in the making of international trade policy. It revealed the potential, but also the problems, for future negotiations on services. The main problem is that many service industries even in developed countries may not be eager to liberalize international trade and services. For example, at one point the FTA included an annex on transportation, but fierce opposition by the marine transport industry in the United States forced its withdrawal late in the negotiation. This incident points out the work that remains to be done to convince industry that further liberalization in trade in services is necessary.

### Investment

The FTA included a chapter on investment, which was a basic demand by the United States. As one U.S. official put it: "The bottom line is that if you get a better trade deal, you need a better investment deal too." This statement, although it could have reflected a bargaining strategy by the Americans, more likely was a reflection on the changes that have occurred in the international trade system. Trade and investment (and services) are increasingly linked in the modern international economy, and business people use trade and investment strategies interchangeably to reach foreign markets. Therefore, it is becoming difficult to negotiate trade rules meaningfully without raising issues of investment; indeed, this fact was made clear by the Canadian side when it argued that trade remedy and dispute settlement was essentially an issue of where future investment would be located. Well before the U.S.-Canada negotiation began, the U.S. government had been pressing unsuccessfully for the inclusion of investment on the GATT agenda; consequently, it saw the bilateral negotiation as an opportunity to make headway on this issue.

In areas such as procurement, services, and even dispute settlement, the United States and Canada have a similar trade history and compatible trade policies. This is not true of investment. The United States has maintained an open investment policy for over two hundred years, and although it has some restrictions, mainly in defense and communications, it remains strongly committed to open investment. On the other hand, Canada has experienced high levels of foreign ownership—reaching about 60 percent of total manufacturing industries and 75 percent in energy; as a result, it has experimented with investment controls. In the early 1970s, Canada created the Foreign Investment Review Agency (FIRA) to screen foreign investment, and later adopted the National Energy Program (NEP) that regulated the energy industry. Both policies precipitated clashes with the United States.[14]

In 1984, the election of a Conservative government produced a sharp change in Canadian policy. Prime Minister Mulroney dismantled the NEP, changed the name (and mandate) of FIRA to Investment Canada, and stopped entirely the policy of reviewing new foreign investment. The reason for Mulroney's actions were not only political conviction, but also a change in circumstances. For one thing, the FIRA had a role in bringing about a large drop in foreign investment in Canada, which fell from an average of C$684 million in 1970-75 to C$372 million in 1976-80.[15] Another reason was that by the mid-1980s Canada's status as a host country was in flux, and it was becoming more active in foreign investment. For example, as noted by A. E. Safarian:

> In 1974 our stock of direct investment abroad as a percentage of the foreign-owned stock in Canada was 20%; today it is at least 60% and rising rapidly . . . the increase in this ratio is remarkable. [16]

It was inevitable that investment would be negotiated in the FTA. Nevertheless, Canada resisted including it as long as possible, probably for the tactical reason of encouraging the United States to be more forthcoming on dispute settlement. The resulting agreement pursued much the same strategy as that on services. The investment chapter called for national treatment of foreign business in all new legislation promulgated by the parties, but it grandfathered all existing legislation and policies where restrictions on foreign investment now apply. The national treatment clause provided for a standstill on discriminatory legislation, and since neither the United States or Canada now restricts new investment they cannot do so in the future. This provision has been controversial in Canada because it limits the scope of future government activity, but without that limitation, it is impossible to provide the stable environment business needs for long-term investment. Canadian and American positions on investment and dispute settlement were the same. Both nations claimed that any restriction of its own government policy on these issues would be a "loss of sovereignty," but one nation's sovereignty is another nation's uncertainty.

The investment chapter liberalized the rules Canada will use in the future to screen direct acquisitions (that is, takeovers) by U.S. investors. This feature was controversial on both sides. U.S. policy generally places no restrictions on acquistions, and there was a strongly held view in Congress that the United States should not accept anything less from Canada. An opposing extreme position in Canada was that there should be no change in current Canadian policy, which is to screen all direct acquisitions over C$5 million. The FTA effected a compromise whereby Canada will increase the threshold for direct screening over four years to C$150 million. Furthermore, Canada will phase out screening of indirect acquisitions—that is, the takeover of a U.S. firm with Canadian assets by another U.S. firm—entirely over three years. In the event an indirect acquisition involves a cultural industry (they are completely exempt from the FTA), Canada shall offer to buy the industry at fair market value if it forces divestiture from a U.S. purchaser.

The change in the threshold of direct acquisitions means that Canada will now only screen takeovers involving the largest 500 to 600 firms. The implications of this action are very much in the eye of the beholder. For Canadians who have an interest in minimizing the deal, it can be said that 75 percent of the assets that are now screened will still be reviewable under the FTA. For Americans who have an interest in maximizing the deal, it can be said that the higher threshold removes some 6,900 Canadian firms from screening, which is a reduction of over 90 percent of the firms whose direct acquisition would now be reviewed.[17] In the Agreement, each side got what it needed, if not what it wanted. The Canadians preserved and even legitimized the right to screen takeovers of the major firms among Canadian companies, while the Americans reduced by over 90 percent the capacity of Canadian bureaucrats to hassle prospective U.S. investors.

The investment chapter contained other features, such as a commitment not to place performance requirements on foreign investors (for example, local content, local sourcing, or export performance requirements). Furthermore, it obliged the parties not to restrict recovery of profits and to provide due process on expropriation. Essentially, these features do not change existing policy, which is true of most of the investment chapter, but they do prevent backsliding in the future. Given the recent history of the two countries, these features probably could be viewed as Canadian concessions. The rapid rise of Canadian investment into the United States, however, means that the investment provisions of the FTA could well be a protection to Canada if U.S. policies were to change in the future.

### Financial Services

The chapter on financial services—covering banking, securities, and trust and loan companies—raises many of the same issues as the chapter on investment. Increasing "trade" in financial services is really a matter of increasing investment, since direct investment is the principal means for firms in one jurisdiction to do business with customers in another. The movement of capital (particularly long-term equity investment) and the right to establish are therefore key considerations in any liberalization of financial services.

The initial positions of Canada and the United States on financial services were very different. For some years, the United States has provided national treatment in the securities industry through a series of bilateral treaties, and in 1978, the International Banking Act established national treatment in the U.S. banking industry. As a result of these policies, foreign banks and securities dealers have the same access to the U.S. market as do U.S. firms. In Canada, however, the financial services sector has been less open to foreign competition. Foreign banks are subject to legal and regulatory restrictions that reduce their capacity to compete fully in the Canadian market. Until recently, the same situation applied in the securities industry, but in December 1986, the government of Ontario announced sweeping changes of securities regulations that will open up the most important securities market in Canada to foreign competition. Because this move also liberalized the industry, it will give U.S. firms operating in Canada wider opportunities than they now have in the United States.

The goal of the United States in the financial services negotiation was to secure national treatment in Canada, particularly in the banking sector. U.S. officials had prepared a study of the treatment of U.S. banks in foreign financial markets that concluded that Canada accorded foreign banks the worst treatment within the G-7 countries.[18] This situation was contrasted with the strong position Canadian banks had established in the United States; for example, in 1985 Canadian bank assets in the United States were about US$40 billion (in comparison with U.S. bank assets in Canada of about C$11.8 billion), and constituted the third-largest foreign presence behind the United Kingdom and Japan.[19] U.S. negotiators were disturbed by the appearance of an internationally aggressive Canadian banking industry operating behind protective barriers in its own domestic market. On the Canadian side, the goal was to forestall any protectionist backsliding in the United States, particularly through congressional reciprocity legislation whereby foreign banks would be accorded the same treatment in U.S. markets that their governments accorded to U.S. banks operating in their jurisdiction.

The agreement on financial services provides more open access to the Canadian market for U.S. banks and financial institutions. U.S. commercial bank subsidaries will be exempt from current restrictions on market share, asset growth, and capital expansion, and they will be able to acquire securities firms and trust companies, as Canadian banks can now do. The 16 percent ceiling on the foreign bank share of total domestic banking assets will not apply to U.S. banks, and rules restricting nonresident shareholders will be relaxed for U.S. banks and for U.S. insurance companies as well. For its part, the United States agreed—in the event of mergers between Canadian banks and securities firms—to permit Canadian banks operating in the United States to underwrite and deal in Canadian government securities. The United States also agreed to extend to Canada any benefits that might accrue from future changes to banking regulations (specifically the Glass-Steagall Act); moreover, it guaranteed that Canadian banks would retain their multistate branches in the United States, which is a benefit not enjoyed by the American banks and which was scheduled for review and possible revocation.

The financial services chapter was an adjunct to the FTA; it was negotiated separately by the U.S. Department of the Treasury and the Canadian Department of Finance. Although the Agreement breaks new ground in that financial services have not previously been included in trade agreements, it nevertheless was not a substantial departure from the status quo. In terms of actual changes to legislation, Canada appears to have done more than the United States, but the U.S. market for financial services was more open than Canada's to begin with. The changes made by Canada are not dramatic, and the remaining protections in Canadian law—plus the sheer commercial strength of Canada's largest banks— ensure that Canada's control of its own financial system will not be endangered. The main result of the Agreement was to secure enough liberalization in Canada to deflect protectionist pressure against Canadian financial institutions in the United States.

### Energy

The energy chapter of the FTA could be described as both conventional and pathbreaking. It is conventional in that it seeks to apply GATT rules, which have been around since 1947, to trade in energy products. It is pathbreaking because nations have effectively ignored those rules in the energy sector in the past. The energy chapter covers an enormous trade volume, which is more than C$10 billion per year and consists mostly of Canadian exports to the United States.

Energy has a high profile for both countries, and it has produced the sharpest trade disputes of the past decade between Washington and Ottawa. It has also stimulated some of the sharpest criticism of the FTA on both sides, and especially in Canada. For a long time, energy trade between the United States and Canada was conducted in the context of plentiful energy resources. Canada sought to export to the United States, while the United States—itself a strong producer of energy resources— restricted imports from Canada in order to protect domestic suppliers. The U.S. policies included import quotas on oil; regulations preventing the marketing of Canadian hydroelectric power; denial of access to enrichment facilities, which impeded Canadian exports of uranium; and maintenance of artificially low prices on natural gas, which denied Canadian producers access to the U.S. market.[20]

In the 1970s, as a result by the Arab oil embargo, energy resources were in short supply and exporters suddenly held the upper hand in energy trade. Canada responded to this situation by adopting policies restricting exports to the United States; this promoted Canada's energy security and, by restricting supply, increased prices in the United States. These policies included a temporary cutback in oil exports in the early 1970s; a two price system which forced U.S. consumers to pay higher prices for oil than domestic consumers; a limitation on electricity exports, which again produced higher prices in the United States; and a reduction of foreign investment in the energy sector.[21]

In sum, energy trade between Canada and the United States was an example of the competitive, self-serving relationships that can develop between exporters and importers in the absence of a long-range agreement to govern that relationship. When resources are readily available, importers deny market access and thereby reduce the capacity for long-range planning and management of the resource in producing countries. When resources are in short supply, exporters deny access to the product, and thereby worsen the problems of managing a shortfall in consuming countries. Obviously, neither side is immune to the uncertainties of the market, but governments on both sides have often acted to make those uncertainties much worse. The energy chapter was an attempt to reduce those uncertainties in U.S.-Canadian trade in oil, natural gas, electricity, and uranium.

What does the FTA do on energy trade? On the importing side, first, it removes all import duties on energy products. This concession was particularly important for Canada, which had long sought a reduction of U.S. tariffs on petrochemicals because they hampered Canada's ability to develop its petrochemical industries, especially in the West. Second, the FTA treats energy like a normal product in Canada-U.S. trade, as is clear from the similarity of wording of articles in the energy chapter with those in Chapter 4 dealing with border measures that apply to all products. Specifically, the FTA mandates that GATT disciplines apply on energy products, which rules out the use of quantitative restrictions and minimum import pricing, and places constraints on internal price control measures.[22] Third, the FTA tightens the exceptions to free trade that are allowed for reasons of national security, which incidentially bears on exports of energy products as well as imports.

On the exporting side, the FTA prohibits taxes on energy exports that do not bear equally on those products destined for domestic consumption. Second, the Agreement follows the GATT in allowing either country to cut back exports when supplies are short or when needed to conserve a finite energy resource, but those actions are permitted only if the cutbacks do not reduce the proportion of total supply previously available to the other country. Furthermore, the exporting country may not set a higher price for exports than for domestic sales. The FTA does not force nations to export, nor does it prevent governments from regulating or restricting exports ahead of time to conserve resources. It does, however, state that once trade is established it cannot be cut back discriminatorily in the short run. In other words, FTA mandates that the market access the importer is obliged to provide in good times is traded off against the access to resources (in the same proportion) the exporter is obliged to provide in bad times.

The energy accord comes at a time of rapid change in international energy trade, especially oil trade. Exporting countries are scrambling for markets and recognize that they need reliable customers. Nations like Venezuela and Saudi Arabia have established joint ventures with firms like Citgo and Texaco to establish an interest in refining and marketing systems in the United States.[23] These agreements have carved up the market and set up commitments between producers and consumers. The motivation behind the FTA energy deal was identical to the motivation behind similar deals occurring elsewhere in the trading world. The main advantage of the FTA energy deal for Canada is that it provides the assured access to markets necessary to attract the large investments needed to exploit Canada's inaccessible and high-cost energy reserves. And for the United States, the deal promises to improve its energy security. For both countries, the other country represents a better trading partner in an energy deal than the alternatives they might have to choose from in the future.

The energy chapter of the FTA has been severely criticized in Canada, with opponents claiming it would mandate a sell-off of Canada's energy resources to the United States. This is simply untrue. The articles in the energy chapter—like the articles in the GATT itself—deal with the movement of goods, not the production of goods. Canada is not required to share energy resources that are not already commercialized and traded. Canada's obligations under the FTA are less than the oil-sharing agreement Canada has entered into under the International Energy Agency. Provincial and even federal surplus tests and other resource management policies are not ruled out by the FTA, and Canada—despite U.S. insistence—made no changes on existing regulations limiting investment by foreigners in the energy sector. The FTA is consistent with long-standing Canadian policy, and as noted by Canadian economist Murray Smith, "The [FTA] energy trade provisions parallel the sectoral proposals made by Canada during the Tokyo Round of GATT negotiations."[24] The energy chapter is one of the most self-balancing chapters of the FTA, and if the FTA should be rejected, it is probable that any subsequent Canadian government would seek to renegotiate it as a sectoral agreement.

## Chapter 5
# Conclusion:
# Should Canada Ratify the FTA?

The FTA was completed before the January 3, 1988, deadline imposed by the U.S. fast-track legislation. The focus then shifted from the diplomats to the legislators. In both countries, it was necessary to draft legislation to implement the Agreement. The implementation phase was not expected to go easily in either country, and particularly in the United States. Under fast-track procedures, Congress cannot make amendments to the Agreement, but this does not prevent individual congressmen from introducing into implementing legislation matters that could affect the deal. Furthermore, the FTA was expected to be on the congressional timetable at the same time as the Omnibus Trade bill, which was the subject of sharp controversy between Congress and the administration. Many thought that Congress might hold the FTA hostage in the bargaining over broader trade legislation—a discouraging scenario reminiscent of the situation that resulted in the narrow agreement in the Senate Finance Committee that began the U.S.-Canadian negotiation.

In Canada, implementation was expected to be less problematic. The Mulroney government had an absolute majority in the Commons, and its electoral mandate did not expire until September 1989. The government's timetable called for passage of implementing legislation by mid-August, after which it would be sent to the Canadian Senate for routine approval. There was a possibility that the province of Ontario would raise a court challenge on the grounds that the federal government had usurped provincial jurisdiction in signing the Agreement. This possibility evaporated, however, when the province became aware of the risk that a court might end up deciding that provinces have little role in trade policy: such a decision would call into question the extensive federal-provincial cooperation that developed during the free trade negotiation.[1]

In the end, congressional implementation of the FTA went smoothly.[2] Meanwhile, a problem arose in Canada that was almost wholly unpredictable. The two Canadian opposition parties had been opposed to the FTA, and if one or both won an election they could repudiate the Agreement. The popularity of free trade in Canada, however, seemed to make the likelihood this would occur remote. Then, without warning, John Turner, the leader of the Liberal party, announced he would call upon all Liberal party members of the Canadian Senate to refuse passage of the implementing legislation in an attempt to force an election on the issue. In one stroke, this transformed the FTA into a domestic political crisis, and possibly a constitutional crisis as well.

There is no basis for Turner's action in modern parliamentary practice in Canada. The Senate is an appointed body, and given the long tenure of Liberal governments in recent years, Liberals constitute a large majority of its members. According to custom, the Senate has the power to debate and possibly to delay legislation, but not to defeat it. It is unknown at this writing what the reaction of the Mulroney government will be to this gambit, and more importantly, what the reaction of the Canadian people will be should an election be called. This action has created enormous political uncertainty, which is something Canadians tend to associate more with the U.S. Congress than with the Canadian political system. What this incident points out is that politics in democratic countries, no matter what the structure, have the potential to be unpredictable. It is this potential for upredictability that the FTA is trying to reduce for the business community on both sides of the border.

Electoral mathematics in Canada do not favor the FTA. For the Agreement to survive an election, Mulroney's Conservatives would have to win a second consecutive majority government (that is, a majority of the seats in Parliament), which has not occurred in Canada since the early 1950s. If the Conservatives fail to win an absolute majority, the Liberals and National Democratic party, which also oppose the FTA, would be able to join together to form a government to reject it.

For the United States, economically, a Canadian rejection would represent an inconvenience and a lost opportunity; politically, in terms of U.S. international trade policy, it would be a more serious embarrassment. In addition, rejection would unquestionably chill U.S. enthusiasm for further trade negotiations with Canada, and enthusiasm was not high to begin with.

For Canada, rejection of the FTA would have more harmful consequences. The FTA has strong political support in the western provinces, Quebec, and most eastern provinces. If the Liberals and/or NDP were to reject the FTA based on a government drawn disproportionately from Ontario, which has more than one-third of parliamentary seats, it would greatly worsen regional alienation in Canada. Rejection would also leave Canada's trade policy in disarray. Freer trade with the United States is a policy that has been pursued for the past decade by Canadian governments from two political parties, by the Foreign Affairs Committee of the Senate, and by an independent Royal Commission. Rejection of Canada-U.S. free trade at this point would necessitate a fundamental reassessment of Canada's international trade policy, but it is not clear where such a reassessment would lead.

One great strength of the FTA is that it is based on economic realism. The reality of Canada's trade position is bilateral. With over three-fourths of Canada's trade going to the United States, Canada is less a multilateral trader than it is a bilateral trader. The reason Canada negotiated bilaterally is because a bilateral agreement had the potential to address more Canadian issues than would a multilateral agreement. Furthermore, Canada has a complex, multifaceted economic relationship with the United States that could only be effectively regulated by a complex, multifaceted agreement.

In international trade diplomacy, trade agreements follow trade. Canada sought a trade agreement with the United States because the United States is the only nation with which it could make a trade agreement that would provide it with objective benefits. For example, theoretically it would be possible for Canada to negotiate a bilateral agreement with the European Community that permitted temporary entry for business persons, or lowered petrochemical tariffs, or provided opportunities to bid on government contracts. Compared to a similar agreement negotiated with the United States, where trade volumes are very much greater, however, such an agreement would have very little practical significance. Even GATT multilateral negotiations do not address Canada's unique concerns. For example, the GATT subsidies code negotiated in the Tokyo Round is a valuable instrument, but it simply does not provide the disciplines on U.S. contingency protection that are mandated by the dispute settlement chapters of the FTA.

Liberal party members in Canada have claimed that, if the FTA is rejected, a Liberal government would negotiate several free trade deals with other countries, to avoid putting all your "eggs in one basket."[3]

But given how much of Canada's trade is with the United States, it seems doubtful such a strategy would serve any real Canadian interest. Worse yet, much of Canada's non-U.S. exports consist of agricultural or resource products, and it is unlikely such trade could form the basis of a free trade agreement acceptable to Canada. For example, when the Trudeau government sought to negotiate a "Contractual Link" with the EC in the early 1970s, the EC mainly wanted lower Canadian tariffs on European exports of manufactured goods in return for greater access to Canadian resources such as uranium ore. This proposal would have relegated Canada to the role of producer of raw materials, and the Canadian government was unwilling to negotiate on this basis. The fact is that the United States represents a quality customer for Canada, and it absorbs most of Canada's high value-added exports of manufactured products. For this reason, the United States is a more appropriate candidate for a trade agreement with Canada than any other nation.

The most important effect of a rejection of the FTA would be on Canada's future relations with the United States. Canada has an exposed trading position with the United States because more than three-fourths of Canada's exports go to the United States, but those exports constitute only about one-fifth of U.S. total imports. Were Canada a company, and equally dependent on sales to a single, larger firm, it would immediately recognize the value of having its relationship secured by a long-term contract. The FTA in effect constitutes just such a contract. It ensures that the United States will treat Canada on a preferential basis consistent with the importance the U.S. market has for Canadian exporters. Without the FTA, the United States would be free to apply multilateral trade policy to Canada, such as it did in August 1971 when President Nixon slapped an import surcharge on all U.S. imports, including those from Canada. A similar action today would seriously threaten Canada's economic welfare, and an FTA provides the only real hope that the United States would make an exception for Canada. In the absence of the FTA, Canada will be in the least-attractive position possible: it will still be heavily dependent on sales to the U.S. market, but its economic relationship with the United States would not be secured. It is a situation with a potential for instability that would not be good for either country.

An additional problem is that U.S. trade policy may not stand still in the event Canada repudiates the FTA. The United States is on record as favoring bilateral or regional free trade agreements, and it has already negotiated a bilateral agreement with Israel. Moreover, the United States is now engaged in advance planning for a free trade agreement with Japan, and formal studies of this proposal are being conducted by the U.S. International Trade Commission and Japan's foreign ministry and Ministry of International Trade and Industry (MITI).[4] It would be deeply ironic if Canada were to reject a bilateral trade agreement only to have the United States turn around and negotiate a similar deal with Japan. This is entirely possible, for as David Owen of the *Financial Times* has noted: "Its [the FTA] progress is being monitored closely around the world. The deal is seen . . . as a possible blueprint for similar bilateral deals between other parties."[5]

Any free trade deal between the United States and Japan could have negative consequences for Canada. For example, if Americans had completely free access to Japanese automotive products, there is some question about whether Canada could maintain its current export volumes of automotive products to the United States. It is interesting to speculate how a new Canadian government that had turned down a free trade agreement with the United States might react if Japan and the United States concluded such an agreement. The most likely scenario is that such a government would find the situation very alarming.

The FTA was produced by a negotiation, and in negotiations nations always proceed on the basis of achieving goals and minimizing losses. One of the goals of the FTA was to increase the competitive environment of Canadian business and international trade. It is a goal the Mulroney government has tried to achieve since its earliest days, and the pursuit of such a goal was strongly supported by the Macdonald Royal Commission as well. The FTA was also designed to avoid certain problems that Canada faces in its trade relations with the United States. If the Agreement is repudiated, these matters will once again be on the agenda, and the new government will have to deal with them.

In the auto sector, as already noted, Canada's duty remission programs will probably produce a bilateral dispute in the absence of the FTA. Beyond this, there could also be a problem with the Auto Pact, which provides for free trade in automotive products. Unfortunately, the mechanism put in place by the pact is unbalanced. On the American side, free trade means that customers, dealers, and manufacturers can buy automotive goods duty free from Canada. On the Canadian side, however, the only parties that receive duty-free treatment are "qualifying" manufacturers (that is, manufacturers that make about as many cars in Canada as they sell there). If ordinary Canadian consumers want to buy a North American automobile, they must buy it from a "qualifying" Canadian company (for example, General Motors Canada) or pay the import duty, and they may not import a used car from the United States at all. These provisions protect Canadian manufacturers, but given that Canada has had a strong surplus on auto trade with the United States, many Americans feel that these safeguards for the Canadian industry are now no longer necessary.

If the FTA is rejected, the United States might seek to renegotiate the Auto Pact, but such a move would be strongly resisted in Canada. As a result, pressures could increase for the United States simply to repudiate the Agreement. The United States would not do so lightly, since the main reason it negotiated the Auto Pact in the first place was to avoid a trade conflict with Canada. But if Canada rejects the FTA, it would weaken U.S. reluctance to take a harmful action against Canada.

Other areas where the FTA resolved potential difficulties in Canada-U.S. economic relations include financial services, liquor board practices, and energy. On the first, it is clear that the access to the U.S. market enjoyed by Canadian banks is not reciprocated for U.S. banks in Canada. In the absence of the FTA, the United States might try to deal with this disparity through reciprocity legislation. If it did so, Canadian banking operations in the United States might be damaged. Regarding liquor board practices, loss of the FTA would mean that the United States would no longer have an incentive to remain aloof from the GATT proceedings launched by the EC against Canada. Were the United States to actually support the Europeans, it would increase the difficulty this issue presents for Canada. Finally, on energy, the FTA helped achieve market access to the United States for Canada's energy producers. If the Agreement is overturned, Ottawa could well be pressed to show how it could develop markets for Canadian energy through other policies.

There are some in Canada who believe the FTA was a radical departure in Canadian trade policy and in Canada's relationship with the United States. This is not the case. The FTA was distinctive in that it packaged a large number of issues, but the issues themselves have been the subjects of Canadian trade policy in the past. Nor was the FTA a departure from the ordinary discourse of Canadian-U.S. economic relations. For Canada, one advantage of negotiating the FTA was to package issues together to get the decisionmaking attention of the U.S. administration, and to get bargaining credit for changing some things (like liquor board pricing policies) that Canada would probably have to change anyway. Removing the FTA does not remove the issues that were included within it. Rather, it ensures that those issues will be taken up later in a more piecemeal and less organized process—and such a process will be less advantageous to Canadian interests than the FTA would have been.

The FTA has been attacked in Canada in extremely emotional terms. Opponents have argued it will destroy the Canadian nation, or lead to the "castration" of Canadian culture. Such claims seem simply preposterous when measured against the language and impact of modern international trade agreements. International trade agreements, including the FTA, are cautious documents negotiated by cautious bureaucrats; if they are bold or imaginative, they are so only within a narrow and circumscribed framework. International trade agreements, including the FTA, more often codify existing government practices than change those practices, and they do not have a revolutionary impact on the nations that enter into them. The proof of this statement is that in Canada the business community, on whom the FTA will have the greatest immediate impact, is largely supportive of the Agreement. If it were otherwise, given the importance that business constitutents typically have in the making of modern trade agreements, the FTA would never have been concluded.

The FTA is a magnet in Canada for those who oppose modern economic life and for those who oppose the preponderant presence of the United States in Canadian life. Neither the effects of modern economic life nor American influence will be reduced by rejecting the FTA. In all nations today, people are facing the internationalization of the domestic economy, as well as increased competition on a world scale. These changes are painful, but they are not a result of the FTA or any other trade agreement. Instead, the FTA is an intelligent response to these pressures because by removing trade protectionism it removes incentives to be inefficient.

As for the American presence, it is undeniable that it creates pressure on Canadian culture and possibly on Canadian political independence as well. But these pressures are not substantially increased by improving Canada's ability to compete economically with the United States, such as the FTA tariff deal will do; or by reaching complementary agreements based on self-interest, such as the FTA energy deal will accomplish. The FTA was intended to strengthen Canada's economy, not (at least directly) to preserve its culture or to protect its independence. But in the modern age, a nation's culture and its political independence are mainly protected by the vitality of its economy. If the FTA strengthens Canada's economy—and there is a widespread belief that it will—then it will increase the strength of the Canadian nation in numerous other ways as well.

# Notes

## Chapter 1

1. Simon S. Reisman, "The Issue of Free Trade," in Edward R. Fried and Philip H. Trezise, eds., *U.S.-Canadian Economic Relations: Next Steps?* (Washington, D.C.: Brookings Institution, 1984), pp. 35-51.

2. Sperry Lea, *A Canada-U.S. Free Trade Agreement: Survey of Possible Choices* (Washington, D.C., and Montreal: Canadian-American Committee, 1963), p. 85.

3. J. L. Granatstein, "Free Trade between Canada and the United States: The Issue that Will Not Go Away," in Denis Stairs and Gilbert R. Winham, eds., *The Politics of Canada's Economic Relationship with the United States* (Toronto: University of Toronto Press, 1985), pp. 11-54.

4. Canada, House of Commons, *Debates,* vol. 1 (1878), pp. 854, 862.

5. Craufurd D. W. Goodwin, *Canadian Economic Thought: The Political Economy of a Developing Nation 1814-1914* (Durham, N.C.: Duke University Press, 1961), esp. pp. 53-59.

6. *A Review of Canadian Trade Policy* (Ottawa: Department of External Affairs, 1983), pp. 5-6.

7. Gilbert R. Winham, "The Canadian Automobile Industry and Trade-Related Performance Requirements," *Journal of World Trade Law,* vol. 18, no. 6 (November-December 1984), pp. 471-96.

8. Philip H. Trezise, "At Last, Free Trade with Canada?" *The Brookings Review,* vol. 6, no. 1 (Winter 1988), pp. 16-23.

## Chapter 2

1. This point was made vividly in the work of Harold Innis, who argued that Canada's boundaries and internal settlement patterns were largely determined by the fur trade. Harold A. Innis, *The Fur Trade in Canada: An Introduction to Canadian Economic History* (Toronto: University of Toronto Press, 1927).

2. Reisman, "Issue of Free Trade," p. 4.

3. See Gary Clyde Hufbauer, "Subsidy Issues After the Tokyo Round," in William R. Cline, ed., *Trade Policy in the 1980s* (Washington, D.C.: Institute

for International Economics, 1983), Table 10.1, p. 328. Also, Moroz has commented as follows about Canadian subsidies: "Between 1971 and 1980, the nominal and the real value of grants paid to domestic industries under current subsidy programs alone grew by over 375 percent and by over 225 percent respectively. . . ." Andrew R. Moroz, "Some Observations on Non-Tariff Barriers and Their Use in Canada," in John Whalley, ed., *Canada-United States Free Trade,* vol. 11, Royal Commission on the Economic Union and Development Prospects for Canada (Toronto: University of Toronto Press, 1985), p. 246.

4. Canada, House of Commons, *Debates,* vol. 3 (1904), p. 4351.

5. *Report of the Royal Commission on the Economic Union and Development Prospects for Canada,* vol. 1 (1985), p. 263.

6. Ibid., vol. 2, p. 411.

7. Ibid., pp. 411-12.

8. Ibid., p. 52.

9. Ibid., vol. 1, pp. 62, 66.

10. Ibid., vol. 2, p. 200.

11. Ibid., vol. 1, pp. 62-63.

12. Ibid., vol. 2, p. 200.

13. Ibid., p. 201.

14. *Competitiveness and Security: Directions for Canada's International Relations* (Ottawa: Department of External Relations, 1985).

15. Ibid., p. 43.

16. Gilbert R. Winham, *International Trade and the Tokyo Round Negotiation* (Princeton: Princeton University Press, 1986), pp. 280-302.

17. David Leyton-Brown, *Weathering the Storm: Canadian-U.S. Relations, 1980-83* (Toronto: Canadian-American Committee, 1985).

## Chapter 3

1. *A Review of Canadian Trade Policy* and *Canadian Trade Policy for the 1980s: A Discussion Paper* (Ottawa: Department of External Affairs, 1983).

2. Gary C. Hufbauer and Andrew J. Samet, "U.S. Response to Canadian Initiatives for Sectoral Trade Liberalization, 1983-84," in Denis Stairs and Gilbert R. Winham, eds., *The Politics of Canada's Economic Relationship with the United States,* vol. 29 of research program of the Royal Commission on the Economic Union and Development Prospects for Canada (Toronto: University of Toronto Press, 1985).

3. *How to Secure and Enhance Canadian Access to Export Markets* (Ottawa: Department of External Affairs, January 1985).

4. See I. M. Destler, *American Trade Politics: System Under Stress* (Washington, D.C.: Institute for International Economics/The Twentieth Century Fund, 1986).

5. "The Senators Relent" (Editorial), Toronto *Globe and Mail,* April 24, 1986.

6. The United States recognized the importance of the Canadian provinces in trade matters, and included provincial ratification of an agreement as one

of its early demands. See Jennifer Lewington, "Reagan Outlines Wish-list for Talks about Free Trade," Toronto *Globe and Mail*, April 29, 1986.

7. *Canada-U.S. Trade Negotiations: A Chronology* (Ottawa: Government of Canada, undated).

8. Christopher Waddell, "Preliminary Round of Free-trade Talks Expected to Be Finished in Two Months," Toronto *Globe and Mail*, July 31, 1986.

9. Giles Gherson, "'Vision Lacking' in Reagan Push for Free Trade Pact," Toronto *Financial Post*, June 14, 1986.

10. Giles Gherson, "Divided U.S. Front Slowing Trade Negotiator's Efforts," Toronto *Financial Post*, June 28, 1986.

11. Christopher Waddell, "U.S. Ambassador Defends Cedar Duty as Protecting Jobs," Toronto *Globe and Mail*, May 29, 1986.

12. William Mackness, "My View: Dispute Settlement Key to Free Trade," Toronto *Financial Post*, July 19, 1986.

13. Lansing Lamont, "A Trade War with Canada?" *The New York Times*, November 17, 1986.

14. For example, the Toronto *Globe and Mail*, normally supportive of closer Canada-U.S. trade relations, titled its editorial on this subject "A Bully's Victory," January 3, 1987.

15. Christopher Waddell, "U.S. to Dictate how Ottawa Can Aid Lumber Firms," Toronto *Globe and Mail*, January 2, 1987.

16. Jennifer Lewington, "U.S. 'Wish List' on Services Trade Politically Difficult," Toronto *Globe and Mail*, December 3, 1986.

17. Alan Bass, "'Weak' Industries and the Auto Pact Reported Abandoned in Trade Talks," Toronto *Globe and Mail*, February 26, 1987. This story was reportedly based on a leak by Reisman himself.

18. For example: "Ms. Carney [Patricia Carney, Canadian minister of international trade] said that, when Canadian negotiator Simon Reisman evaluates instruments for resolving disputes, he uses the softwood lumber controversy as his touchstone." John Cruickshank, "Free-trade Talks Approach Make-or-break Point," Toronto *Globe and Mail*, June 26, 1987.

19. Christopher Waddell, "Investment Issue Now Adding to Difficulties in Trade Talks," Toronto *Globe and Mail*, May 21, 1987.

20. "Americans 'Led Us On,' Reisman Says," Toronto *Globe and Mail*, September 28, 1987.

21. Giles Gherson, "Reagan's Signal Brings Trade Talks out of Obscurity," Toronto *Financial Post*, February 2, 1987.

22. See *Canada-U.S. Trade Negotiations*.

23. Christopher Waddell and Jennifer Lewington, "Canada, U.S. Plan Bid to Salvage Trade Talks," Toronto *Globe and Mail*, September 28, 1987. Later Ambassador Yeutter returned this impoliteness by claiming that " . . . had Canada not selected Mr. Reisman as their chief negotiator, we would have had this agreement six months ago." Jennifer Lewington, "Reisman Was Negative Force, Key U.S. Trade Official Says," Toronto *Globe and Mail*, October 6, 1987.

24. Graham Fraser, "PM Warns of 'Tough Business' If an Accord Not Achieved," Toronto *Globe and Mail,* September 26, 1987.

25. Giles Gherson and Hyman Solomon, "Trade Talks: Touch and Go," Toronto *Financial Post,* September 21-27, 1987.

26. Jennifer Lewington and Christopher Waddell, "Hopes for Trade Deal Nearing End," Toronto *Globe and Mail,* October 2, 1987.

27. Jennifer Lewington and Christopher Waddell, "U.S. Reported to Accept Key Trade Demand," Toronto *Globe and Mail,* October 3, 1987.

28. Jennifer Lewington and Christopher Waddell, "Late Push by Baker Shows Reagan Wish for Canadian Pact," Toronto *Globe and Mail,* October 5, 1987.

29. See Canada-U.S. Free Trade Agreement, *Elements of the Agreement,* preliminary transcript (Ottawa: Government of Canada, undated).

30. See Rodney de C. Grey, *Trade Policy in the 1980s: An Agenda for Canadian-U.S. Relations* (Montreal: C.D. Howe Institute, 1981).

31. *Report of the Task Force on Program Review,* Neilsen report (Ottawa: Supply and Services, 1986). The Neilsen report characterized federal and provincial tax incentives, grants, and subsidies to Canadian business as "giving with both hands," p. 6.

32. In return, the United States has argued that if subsidies are not significant, then material injury will be harder to demonstrate, with the result that countervailing duties will be disallowed.

33. The legislation implementing this agreement explicitly prohibited any devolution from existing U.S. trade remedy legislation.

34. For example, *Directory of Incentives for Business Investment and Development in the United States,* National Association of State Development Agencies (Washington, D.C.: Urban Institute Press, 1986).

35. Remarks by Gary Horlick in Murray G. Smith and Frank Stone, eds., *Assessing the Canada-U.S. Free Trade Agreement* (Ottawa: Institute for Research on Public Policy, 1987), p. 116. Horlick continued: "Our subsidies go through tax refinancing and tax holidays and free land in the states. When we go out and want a Toyota plant, it's not the federal government, it's the State of Kentucky, which even flew workers to Japan for training. There are plenty of subsidies, they're just not so obvious."

36. Winham, *International Trade and the Tokyo Round Negotiation* (Princeton: Princeton University Press, 1986), p. 392.

## Chapter 4

1. Technically, the GATT applies to energy, but effective trade regulation in this sector has been conducted outside the GATT.

2. Debra P. Steger, "An Analysis of the Dispute Settlement Provisions of the Canada-U.S. Free Trade Agreement," Paper prepared for the Business Council on National Issues, Ottawa, undated, p. 19.

3. Alan M. Rugman and Andrew D. M. Anderson, *Administered Protection in America* (London: Croom Helm, 1987), pp. 79, 85.

4. Gary N. Horlick and Sheila J. Landers, "The Free Trade Agreement Working Group: Developing a Harmonized and Improved Countervailing Duty Law," Paper presented to the American Bar Association National Institute, January 29, 1988.

5. Simon Reisman, "The Nature of the Canada-U.S. Trade Agreement," in Murray G. Smith and Frank Stone, eds., *Assessing the Canada-U.S. Free Trade Agreement* (Ottawa: Institute for Research on Public Policy, 1987), p. 43.

6. Jeffrey J. Schott, "The Free Trade Agreement: A U.S. Assessment," in Jeffrey J. Schott and Murray G. Smith, eds., *The Canada-United States Free Trade Agreement: The Global Impact* (Washington, D.C., and Ottawa: Institute for International Economics and Institute for Research on Public Policy, 1988), p. 17.

7. R. A. Jenness, "Canada-U.S. Free Trade: What the Economic Council's Simulations Say," in Smith and Stone, eds., *Assessing the Canada-U.S. Free Trade Agreement,* pp. 201-207.

8. Ibid., p. 205, and Schott and Smith, *Canada-United States Free Trade Agreement: The Global Impact,* p. 18.

9. *Report of the Royal Commission on the Economic Union and Development Prospects for Canada,* vol. 1 (1985), p. 330.

10. Jenness, "Canada-U.S. Free Trade," p. 203.

11. John Whalley, "Economic Regional and Labour Market Adjustment Implications of Canada-U.S. Free Trade," in Smith and Stone, eds., *Assessing the Canada-U.S. Free Trade Agreement,* p. 211.

12. Paul Wonnacott, "The Auto Sector," in Schott and Smith, eds., *Canada-United States Free Trade Agreement,* pp. 101-109.

13. Jeffrey J. Schott and Murray G. Smith, "Services and Investment," in Schott and Smith, eds., *Canada-United States Free Trade Agreement,* p. 137.

14. See David Leyton-Brown, *Weathering the Storm.*

15. Testimony of Steven J. Canner in U.S. Congress, House, Committee on Banking, Finance and Urban Affairs, May 24, 1988, p. 2.

16. A. E. Safarian, "Investment Aspects of the Canada-U.S. Free Trade Agreement," in Smith and Stone, eds., *Assessing the Canada-U.S. Free Trade Agreement,* p. 123.

17. Testimony of Steven J. Canner in U.S. Congress, House, Committee on Banking, Finance and Urban Affairs, May 24, 1988, p. 3.

18. Transcript of remarks by Thomas J. Berger, U.S. Department of Treasury, before the Pace University Institute for U.S.-Canada Business Studies, New York, June 3, 1987.

19. Schott and Smith, "Services and Investment," in *The Canada-United States Free Trade Agreement,* p. 142.

20. Philip K. Verleger, Jr., "Implications of the Energy Provisions," in Schott and Smith, eds., *The Canada-United States Free Trade Agreement,* p. 118.

21. Ibid., p. 117.

22. Minimum import prices would likely be contrary to GATT Article XI:1,

but to leave no doubt the FTA specifically prohibited this practice in Article 902:2.

23. Daniel Yergin, "Big Oil May Never Be the Same," *The New York Times*, June 20, 1988.

24. Murray G. Smith, "The Canada-U.S. Agreement in an International Context," in Smith and Stone, eds., *Assessing the Canada-U.S. Free Trade Agreement*, p. 69.

## Chapter 5

1. Christopher Waddell, "Free-trade Court Challenge Carries Risks for Ontario," Toronto *Globe and Mail*, May 18, 1988.

2. The legislation moved especially quickly in the Senate Finance Committee and the House Ways and Means Committee. As one Finance Committee staffer said: "The bill was done in three weeks. We do *nothing* in three weeks, not even monuments." The speed was due in part to the earlier involvement of Congress in the negotiation, which is mandated by the fast-track procedures. But it also may have been due to exhaustion from the long fight between Congress and the administration over the Omnibus Trade bill.

3. Richard Clerous, "Turner to Offer String of Free-trade Pacts," Toronto *Globe and Mail*, July 27, 1988.

4. Clyde H. Farnsworth, "U.S. and Japan Ponder a Free Trade Proposal," *The New York Times*, August 12, 1988.

5. David Owen, "Free Trade Deal at Mercy of Canadian Voters," London *Financial Times*, August 9, 1988.

# Index